Taking Flight to Literacy
and Leadership!

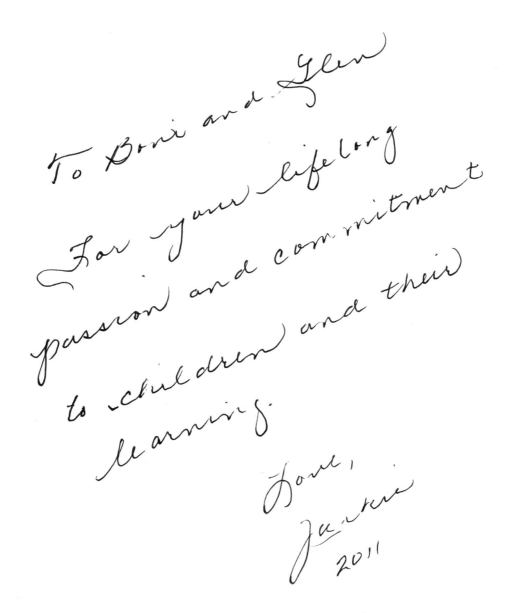

To Boni and Glen

For your lifelong
passion and commitment
to children and their
learning.

Love,
Jackie
2011

Taking Flight to Literacy and Leadership!

Soaring to New Heights in Learning

Jacqueline J. Brayman and Maureen A. Grey
with Michael A. Stearns

*A guide to improving student achievement,
leadership, and literacy in our schools*

Published in partnership with the
American Association of School Administrators

ROWMAN & LITTLEFIELD EDUCATION
A division of
Rowman & Littlefield Publishers, INC
Lanham • New York • Toronto • Plymouth, UK

Published in partnership with the American Association of School Administrators

Published by Rowman & Littlefield Education
A division of Rowman & Littlefield Publishers, Inc.
A wholly owned subsidary of The Rowman & Littlefield Publishing Group, Inc.
4501 Forbes Boulevard, Suite 200, Lanham, Maryland 20706
www.rowmaneducation.com

Estover Road, Plymouth PL6 7PY, United Kingdom

British Library Cataloguing in Publication Information Available

Library of Congress Cataloging-in-Publication Data
Brayman, Jacqueline J., 1949–
Taking flight to literacy and leadership! : soaring to new heights in learning / Jacqueline J. Brayman and Maureen A. Grey.
    p. cm.
Includes bibliographical references and index.
ISBN 978-1-60709-858-4 (cloth : alk. paper)—ISBN 978-1-60709-859-1 (pbk. : alk. paper)—ISBN 978-1-60709-860-7 (electronic)
1. Literacy. 2. Group work in education. 3. Educational leadership. 4. Academic achievement. I. Grey, Maureen A., 1950– II. American Association of School Administrators. III. Title.
LC149.B73 2011
372.6—dc22

                                                          2010029684

The paper used in this publication meets the minimum requirements of American National Standard for Information Sciences—Permanence of Paper for Printed Library Materials, ANSI/NISO Z39.48-1992.

Printed in the United States of America

This book is dedicated

to Jacqueline's husband, Todd,
for laughter, learning, and patience,
and to the memory of Eve Steere.

to Maureen's family, Jeff Grey,
along with JB, Stacy and Nolan, Dan, Sarah, Joe , and Jessica
for their loving support and encouragement.

to Mike's wife, Mary,
for all her support.

Contents

Acknowledgments

Stephen Covey said it best, "We are better together than we are alone." *Taking Flight to Literacy and Leadership!* was able to lift off thanks to the thinking and effort of many bright, talented people. We have been privileged not only to work with the following people, but also to learn with them. It is our collective learning that provides the substance of this book.

We give special thanks to the entire staff of Northview Public Schools. According to Dr. Robert Hill, Executive Director of The Ball Foundation, "Northview is the best representation of a learning organization" he has seen. The staff and administration are zealous learners and risk takers. They have learned that change is inevitable and that conversation is a critical part of their work. They view their role as teaching *and learning.* It is about their work that we write. They provided us with an authentic arena in which to think, inquire, share, and create knowledge.

The former Northview superintendent, Michael Stearns, is our contributing author. Of him, Dr. Hill states, "The reason that Northview was able to make such marked progress is because Stearns is a learner himself." Mike not only wrote for the book but also provided deep insights and ongoing feedback. He was instrumental in creating the Northview story. Stearns' enthusiasm was an energy source throughout the entire project.

We are grateful to The Ball Foundation for challenging us to think about learning in new and different ways. Our years in association with them were filled with critical friendship and new insights. This book is a tribute to the foundation's passion for learning. A special note of gratitude goes to Mary Jo Kuhlman, former Ball Foundation representative, and Dr. Patricia Oldt, former superintendent of schools for their vision in forging the partnership between Northview Public Schools and the foundation. Mary Jo initiated the early work on understanding change and the importance of conversation. Dr. Oldt laid the ground work for learning as an organization.

We give thanks to Kent Intermediate School District, especially Marcia Logie, Assistant Superintendent of Teaching and Learning, and Kevin Konarska, Superintendent, for their gracious hospitality and encouragement. They generously provided a place for collaboration, and shared their resources so that we could put our knowledge to pen. This, in part, is their story too. They were the first in our locale to encourage collaborative effort.

We take our hats off to Joanne Nelson, our editor, who provided us with expert technical editing. She also shared her educator's perspective from which we took great encouragement.

Moss Ingram, writing consultant, supplied feedback which prompted a total reconfiguration of the book. His insights proved invaluable.

Ohio State University kindly processed our survey data; we give special gratitude to Ann Allen, Ph.D., for designating personnel to help us, and to Cheryl Endres for facilitating this relationship.

We were graced with the friendship and encouragement of a technological wizard, Terry Ziemba, who enabled us to think broadly about the book's application.

Paul Schneider, seasoned consultant, provoked our thinking with tough questions and robust feedback.

Jolene Rosser was our graphic artist who put our ideas into pictoral representation. Our innumerable changes never seemed to try her patience.

Michelle VanGeest, typesetter, lent her keen eye for detail and artistry in creating an appealing text.

Tricia Erickson and Dave Tull engaged their art students in vocabulary development in response to the literacy focus at Northview High School. A small sample of that effort is laced throughout the book.

Our work with the following authors' writings challenged our thinking and increased our capacity as professionals: Meg Wheatley, Rich DuFour, Peter Senge, Doug Fisher, Nancy Frey, Tony Wagner, Bob Kegan, Brian McNulty, Tim Waters, Bob Marzano, Deb Wahlstrom, Jim Collins, Michael Fullan, Ron Heifitz, Etienne

Wenger, Hallie Preskill, and Myron K. Rogers. We hold them all in high esteem.

Professional friends became a cheering gallery and sources of wisdom, especially Myra Bradford, Connie Petter, Janice Crawford, Judy Care, Dr. Julia Reynolds, Marcia Logie. A special remembrance is dedicated to Ruthanne Wambold who inspired many students and colleagues to take FLIGHT!

Jacqueline Brayman was continually motivated to write by her sons' commitment to learning. Son Matthew seldom failed to ask, "So how is the book going, Mom?" and Michael mused, "If it makes it any easier to write the tuition check, I love my learning. The day I stop learning is the day I die. When it's time, just bury me in a cap and gown."

The work that culminated in *Taking Flight to Literacy and Leadership!* was made possible, in large part, by G. Carl Ball, founder of The Ball Foundation. Carl was a visionary fascinated with flight. He especially loved the story of the Wright Brothers who had a dream and the persistence and courage to accomplish it.

Carl was troubled by the fact that some students are successful while others are not. Determined to find out why, Carl returned to college upon his retirement from the presidency of Ball Horticultural Company and obtained a teaching certificate. He taught third grade to learn first-hand about the challenges of teaching and learning. He became a relentless advocate for educational equity and instructional excellence.

Carl's foundation's work supported educators across the country in their quest for student success. He challenged schools to teach so that all students could learn. *Taking Flight to Literacy and Leadership!* is a tribute to Carl Ball as it provides a powerful model of "what works" in schools. It captures the story of the partnership between The Ball Foundation and Northview Public Schools in Grand Rapids, Michigan.

Carl Ball served as an inspiration for improving student achievement, especially in literacy. He encouraged all educators to "Take Flight!" for students and literacy. His efforts made a difference from the classroom to the board room. We gratefully acknowledge Carl's contributions and know that his dream continues to light the way for educators and the students they serve.

Introduction

Transformation

I work in schools to share good ideas, and others made them better.
I work in schools to give answers, but I learned that questions had more
    power.
I work in schools to find familiar mindsets, but I learned the most from dif-
    ferences.
I work in schools to do my own thing, and I found the value of community.
I work in schools to create more, yet I found that strength lies in less.
I work in schools to go fast, but I found that slow got me there more quickly.
I work in schools as a teacher, and I found that I must also be a learner.
I work in schools as an administrator, yet I found I must also be a teacher.
I work in schools as the one to stand up front, but I found the view best from
    the back.
I work in schools to lead people, but they were able to lead themselves.
I work in schools to make a difference; I came away a different person.

Celebration from the Rear View Mirror

Almost everyone entertains an idea for writing a book. Everyone, that is, except us—until we recognized the powerful story of a school district's transformation that had taken place before our very eyes. We were struck by all the learning. Not only did students learn well, but the adults and the school system also flourished. We considered it a responsibility to document this story and share it in support of educators everywhere. We offer it as a guide to literacy, system-wide learning, and leadership.

We three authors had been working together as partners representing Northview Public Schools and The Ball Foundation. The big partnership goal was improving student literacy K-12 through the use of data. That intended goal was achieved. But, in order to see clearly *all* the progress that had occurred, we had to gain some distance from the work by way of career changes. Only then were we able to identify the work that the system had actually done. Northview Public Schools had developed its improvement efforts in three fields of work: literacy, adult learning, and systems thinking.

In these fields we created a razor sharp focus on literacy, anchored adult learning at the center of our efforts, and aligned the whole system to learning. As a result, student achievement increased, the staff developed an identity of shared leadership, and the entire school system was transformed into a learning organization.

We could now see the school system's gains not only in terms of measurable progress but also in terms of improving the quality of our professional lives:

- The clarity of the fields of work made life *simpler.* There were only three. Each field had hard and fast boundaries and flexible processes. We could use our own knowledge to make the work the best it could be.

- We developed shared understanding, vocabulary, and practices within these fields of work which made us more *efficient and effective.* We could talk and work well across grade and building levels.

- Our shared purpose united us together in a common effort and built *trust and improved relationships.* Students' learning needs were always the top priority. We all knew what we stood for and counted on each other to get where we were going. Morale was high.

- Our focus eliminated extraneous distractions. That freed us from worry about "doing the right things" and allowed us to *make the most of our time.*

At the outset of the work we were a band of three leaders in a district of 225 staff. By the end of the partnership we were three facilitators in a learning organization of 225 leaders. It was hard to fit everyone into the cockpit to pilot the FLIGHT! but we learned the power of sharing the pilots' seats.

This book makes transparent the insights gained through the partnership of Northview Public Schools and The Ball Foundation, two very different organizations. *Taking Flight to Literacy and Leadership!* suggests the ways the partners learned to increase student achievement, improve literacy instruction, enhance adult learning, and develop systems thinking which result in learning for all and a district's transformation into a learning organization.

Hindsight is Always 20/20

True confessions: Our leadership training had led us to believe that we were supposed to know most of the answers. All of us had studied leadership theories and conscientiously put them into practice. We had served our people, developed visions, cranked out strategic plans, and accomplished enough goals to choke the proverbial ox(en)! We were, for the most part, respected and even occasionally liked. We figured we were good, effective leaders.

We assumed that leaders were responsible to know and understand the challenges staff members face. We knew what our staff needed to learn, we knew their highest priorities, and we knew what structures worked best for getting their jobs done. We spent more time telling, suggesting, and deciding rather than inquiring, listening, and sharing. We knew, we knew, we knew. Our good intentions created the assumption that we were doing the right things. Yet much to our dismay, the improvements we worked so hard to produce often did not come.

It is easy for assumptions to limit our thinking, especially when the demands of the job allow so little time to take the balcony view to see the big picture. Had we venerated staff's knowledge as much as our own, we could have unleashed the energy of adult learning, shared leadership, and the power of systems thinking on our districts. Then *everyone* would have been "at the controls" and all of us could have taken FLIGHT! to increase student achievement.

School administrators have unending demands. In forging our partnership, we wondered, "Is there another way to do this hard work? How might we improve the way we operate to achieve the results we seek? How much better might we do? What would it take to become a healthy, vibrant learning organization?"

We have learned extraordinarily important lessons about leadership through the partnership; however, having a foundation as a partner was not prerequisite to our learning. The Ball Foundation did not come with deep pockets. It came offering the opportunity for Northview to plan and participate in its own learning. The foundation engaged the school system in provocative thought partnership.

As intended, the thought partnership between the foundation and the district frequently gave rise to differing perspectives. Intellectual sparring often ensued that stretched beliefs. One belief, that key instructional decisions needed to be generated by central office, became a point initially for contention, and then for experimentation. With the repeated successful engagement of staff in instructional decision making, the original belief morphed into a new understanding: Genuine participation of all staff in instructional decision making is critical.

Authors Brayman, Grey, and Stearns now emphatically state that, "Unless we share leadership with teachers, improvement work cannot be done." We now regularly spout, "People only support what they create (Wheatley, 1992) or consider meaningful to themselves." The result of putting this principle into action was that everyone in the district can see themselves in this story. The lead authors are conduits for the many to put their learning, change, hard work, and success to the written page.

Our learning in partnership was a journey made possible by the research of many others and the day-to-day work of the Northview staff. It has been said that a journey is more than just a trip. Journeys provide experience that change who we are and how we see the world. We are all very different professionals because of this journey of working and learning together. Everyone now shares the responsibility for the vision and the results. The vision provides the glue that binds us all in common purpose, language, and identity. Results are the responsibility to which we hold ourselves.

Between vision and results sits learning. Learning is truly the engine of the organization. It is constant learning that renders each staff member a potential spark for innovation and a solver of the next challenge. It is the sharing of one learner with the next that expands the capacity of the district to continually improve, and it is the sharing of knowledge that transforms everyone into a leader. With these conditions in place, a district can take FLIGHT!

The external pressures have not waned but our ability to respond effectively has been strengthened. No longer do we band together to cope with the next mandate; instead, we purposefully gather to share our knowledge to "Prepare students for life's next step," Northview's mission statement. Our commitment to insisting upon the participation of all unleashes the collective knowledge in the district for the benefit of each and every staff member and student. This commitment validates everyone's worth and gives us hope and confidence from learning in community.

In the book, key principles of learning will light your way, just as runway lights guide a pilot's safe landing. Given the key principle previously espoused, "People only own what they create," it follows that Northview's model serves simply as that, a model. Other school systems are encouraged to read the story of Northview's transformation and "make it their own." This book is meant to provoke a district's thinking. It is our intent that readers will ask, "Given *our* many strengths, what is possible for *us*? Where can our FLIGHT! take *us*?"

About Us

Between them, authors Jacqueline Brayman, Maureen Grey, and Mike Stearns have worn almost every hat in a school system: student, teacher, parent, consultant, principal, assistant superintendent, superintendent. Our experience is broad and deep, each of us having logged well over thirty years in the profession. Maureen and Mike worked together in the same district, Northview Public Schools, for many years, and Jacqueline kept crossing their respective paths through shared projects at the county level.

Our similar passion for learning drew us into collegial friendship early in our careers. We developed mutual respect for one another based on our shared interests and willingness to take risks. Over time we came to trust each other and developed the candor to tell one another, "the way it is." Jacqueline shifted her work from public education to the private sector with The Ball Foundation which targeted literacy achievement as its primary goal. Serendipitously, this foundation had already forged a partnership with Northview Public Schools to do action research on using data to inform instructional decision making. Jacqueline was assigned to represent the foundation in this partnership.

It seemed that the sun, moon, and stars had lined up, as Mike was Northview's Superintendent and Maureen, the Director of Instruction. Mike was committed to securing a data warehouse for the district. Maureen led the initiative to bring the professional learning communities concept, a model for collaboration, to staff. Northview, in tandem with the foundation, pursued its research on data. With Jacqueline's outside perspective, all of us were able to discover the possible connections between data, teachers' learning and practice, and the potential of the system to be a catalyst for improvement.

We are honored to have worked with students, teachers, and the entire system as they learned together. They worked collectively to create their preferred future and simultaneously transformed the school system into a learning organization. Our expectations of education will never be the same.

PART 1:
FLIGHT! Preparation

This graphic represents the story of Northview Public Schools and its transformation to become a learning organization. It shows the integration of three fields of work—literacy, adult learning, and systems thinking—that results in increased literacy achievement and shared leadership.

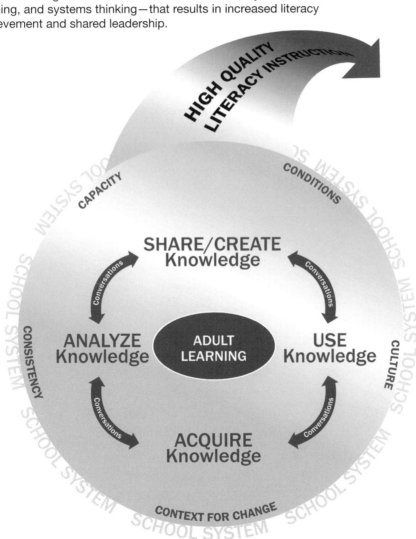

Chapter 1

FLIGHT! Overview

Tough Question:

- What questions provoke learning about student achievement?

Key Learning Principle:

- The questions we ask are often more important than the answers.

Main Ideas:

- Regardless of our role, we share the same goal of increasing student achievement.

- We can start with one identified need as a springboard for building the capacity of the whole school system.

- Data can be a portal for learning how to:

    . . .become expert at literacy instruction K-12
    . . .develop structures and processes for adult learning
    . . .align the entire school system to student and adult learning

$\mathcal{T}$his is a powerful story about a school system that vaulted literacy to its highest priority, determined how adults learn best to improve their practice, and aligned the system to support learning. The result was that student achievement increased, teachers came to see themselves as leaders, and the school system transformed itself into a learning organization.

It is 2 a.m. on a September morning early in the school year, and Superintendent Stearns paces the bedroom floor grappling with a question that continually plagues him: "How do I mobilize the whole school system to improve the achievement of *every* child?" Superintendents, does this sound familiar?

The last vestiges of daylight filter through the office window and middle school principal, Andy Scogg, rocks back in his chair stewing over building priorities, "There are *so* many expectations from both internal and external sources. We can't possibly do everything. Where do we target our energies so that our students can best profit and learn?" Principals, does this sound familiar?

At her kitchen table, Kelly Putnam burns the midnight oil as she second guesses the effectiveness of her lessons plans for 2nd grade language arts tomorrow. "The spread of my students' reading abilities is so wide. Will this lesson engage them all so they gain the needed knowledge? I want to make sure I meet their needs. What else could I do?" Teachers, does this sound familiar?

Director of Instruction, Maureen Grey, anticipates teachers' disappointment as she mulls over students' writing scores on the state assessment. "Our scores spiked two years ago after we focused our professional development on writing. We have had all that time to improve our instruction, so why have some grade level scores declined recently? We've put so much effort into it." Curriculum Directors, does this sound familiar?

The examples in the above paragraphs are mirrors of leaders across the country who share the same end goal of increasing student achievement. In this story administrators demonstrate that an entire school system can learn, grow, and transform itself into a learning organization that meets the learning needs of its students. It is a concrete model of how one district increased student literacy achievement while positively impacting the adult learners and the entire system.

This book is a challenge to formal school leaders everywhere to recognize the power of their positions. Although it is desirable to promote leadership throughout the entire staff, positional leaders are still critical to the growth and progress of the system. It remains their responsibility to develop the vision, and carry its banner. It is their ultimate task to align the work of the district so that the vision can be achieved.

If nothing else, *Taking Flight to Literacy and Leadership!* is a guide for school leaders to leverage their resources so that everyone can do "what matters."

This we know. Student learning is orchestrated from the classroom. But quality instruction that stimulates student learning is facilitated through the efforts of formal leadership. It is one of *the* primary functions of the system. The student must learn to prepare for his future. The teacher must learn about his instructional practice. And the entire system must learn how to support all stakeholders so that they and the system itself can flourish and grow.

Taking Flight to Literacy and Leadership! suggests that district leaders elevate the role of teachers to include learning *and* leading. However, the complex work of the system cannot be led from the classroom. Teachers can lead instructional improvement and learning; they have deep insight into how to improve system practices. However, they must not be saddled with the responsibility of leading the entire system forward. That remains the work of positional leaders so that teachers can focus on teaching and learning.

Paradoxically this book challenges district leaders to both expand and narrow the scope of their work. We are strengthened when we see our work broadly as "systems work" wherein everything is potentially connected and capable of providing information for the next challenge. We are fortified when we focus upon a few powerful points of leverage which we ply to improve and grow our work.

We believe that school systems can start with an identified need as a springboard to building the capacity of the whole school system. No standards exist for the ideal time to begin, but student learning can't wait. Like other districts we worried, "What's the best time to get started?" Over time we learned that the answer is *NOW*, always *NOW!*

Northview's FLIGHT! began with just a simple question. Staff asked, "Should we buy a new reading program, use our old commercial program, or design our own?" Although this process concentrated on choosing the "right" reading program, it revealed the district's limited use of data as a tool for decision making. The quest for answers positioned Northview on the runway to make significant improvements in student achievement and adult learning. It all started with this simple question, but *the bigger question* became, "What does the data show?"

Superintendent Mike Stearns and Director of Instruction Maureen Grey redirected the decision making process. "Let's do an in-depth look at our students' records. Can we find a correlation between reading achievement and other important variables besides our reading series?"

Staff had presumed that students struggling with reading had moved into the district and not profited from long-term Northview instruction. They carefully reviewed student files, one at a time, looking for patterns. Eventually they discovered that the reasons for the delayed reading skills contradicted their original assumptions. This revelation made obvious the value of using data to determine current reality. Having invested untold hours in ferreting out the problem, the staff asked, "How might we be able to obtain data on our students to support our decision making?" This was a defining moment in Northview's learning: *The staff sought improvement by asking a question rather than following assumptions.*

Although staff was tentative about this new way of thinking, they asked another powerful data question: "Is there a practical way to manage a large amount of student data?" Thus, with simple inquiry, Northview began its journey to planning instruction based on data. This ultimately was a catalyst for transforming the school system to a learning organization.

As the Northview FLIGHT! story unfolds, you will learn that using data became the staff's portal for learning how to:

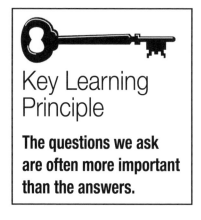

Key Learning Principle

The questions we ask are often more important than the answers.

- become expert at literacy instruction K-12, based upon data.
- develop structures and processes for adult learning.
- align the entire school system to both student and adult learning.

Literacy: Use Data to Become Experts

Northview was able to achieve high levels of literacy achievement because all staff intentionally designated literacy as their "Number One" priority. Through research for their strategic plan, they recognized that one consistent focus would translate into higher achievement.

With a singular focus on literacy, staff aligned district resources to support literacy learning. They funded classroom libraries and procured leveled books. Staff developed a literacy coaching network and a new model of professional development that reframed district activities around "adult learning."

Teacher proficiency grew from the adoption of a K-12 literacy framework and school-wide strategies. Northview's staff came to see themselves as teachers of literacy. No matter the grade level of students or content area, K-12 teachers consistently welcomed and pursued this focus. Over time, this common direction proved invaluable to student achievement K-12.

RESULTS IN LITERACY

As measured by the State of Michigan MEAP (Michigan Educational Assessment Program) test, reading achievement consistently rose. Scores were tracked from 2000—the first year of the Northview-Ball Foundation partnership—to 2008—one year beyond the last year of the formal partnership. The inclusion of 2008 data suggests the sustainability of accomplishments achieved by the focus on literacy, adult learning, and systems work.

For all levels analyzed (Grades 4, 7, and 11), student achievement shows evidence of consistent high levels of proficiency. Despite significantly increased levels of poverty in all of its schools, Northview's students' literacy scores are rising. Data show a solid trend of improving student achievement. Staff's commitment to the literacy focus, in tandem with the work on adult learning and the system, supports continued success.

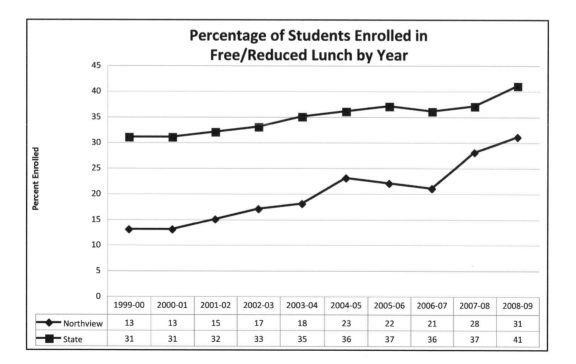

	1999-00	2000-01	2001-02	2002-03	2003-04	2004-05	2005-06	2006-07	2007-08	2008-09
Northview	13	13	15	17	18	23	22	21	28	31
State	31	31	32	33	35	36	37	36	37	41

Scores were analyzed in Grades 4, 7, and 11, designated years that the MEAP tests were administered. Northview's 4th graders, on average, scored 15 percentage points higher than 4th graders statewide. From the early years of the partnership to its conclusion, achievement in reading showed an almost 20 percentage points gain, compared to a gain of approximately 13 percentage points scored by 4th graders statewide. The last five years showed scores for Northview's 4th graders remaining consistently high—ranging from 91-93.8% proficiency.

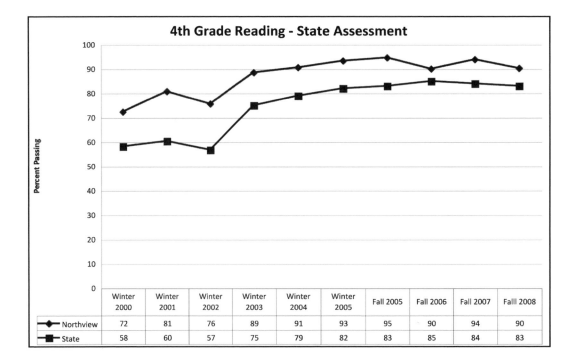

4th Grade Reading - State Assessment

	Winter 2000	Winter 2001	Winter 2002	Winter 2003	Winter 2004	Winter 2005	Fall 2005	Fall 2006	Fall 2007	Falll 2008
Northview	72	81	76	89	91	93	95	90	94	90
State	58	60	57	75	79	82	83	85	84	83

Northview's 7th grade scores showed a similar trend. Despite the fact that middle school scores at the national level typically reflect a downturn, Northview's 7th grade reading scores actually rose. On average, Northview's 7th graders scored approximately 11 percentage points higher than the state's 7th graders. From the outset of the partnership to its conclusion, scores rose 32 percentage points. Given his building's rapidly rising poverty rates, Andy Scogg, Crossroads Middle School principal, terms the achievement gains "extraordinary" compared to state and national averages.

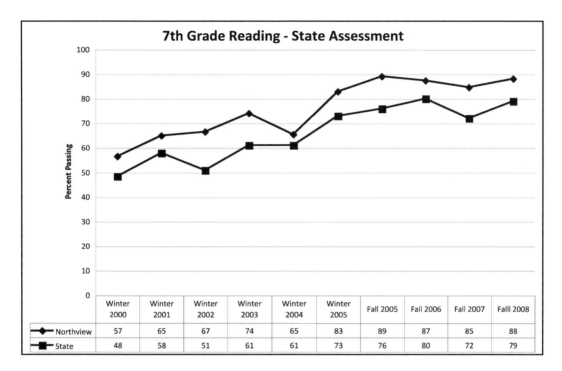

7th Grade Reading - State Assessment

	Winter 2000	Winter 2001	Winter 2002	Winter 2003	Winter 2004	Winter 2005	Fall 2005	Fall 2006	Fall 2007	Falll 2008
Northview	57	65	67	74	65	83	89	87	85	88
State	48	58	51	61	61	73	76	80	72	79

At the 11th grade level, data was analyzed over the partnership years. From 2000-2006, Northview's 11th graders outperformed their statewide peers by 8 percentage points. Though the last year tracked, 2006, showed a modest dip,

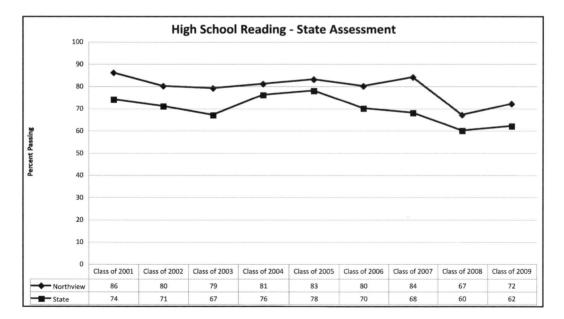

High School Reading - State Assessment

	Class of 2001	Class of 2002	Class of 2003	Class of 2004	Class of 2005	Class of 2006	Class of 2007	Class of 2008	Class of 2009
Northview	86	80	79	81	83	80	84	67	72
State	74	71	67	76	78	70	68	60	62

to 78% proficiency, previous scores remained consistently high in the range from 81% to 86% proficiency. Northview's 11th graders scored higher than the state average every year that scores were tracked. They continue to show high levels of reading achievement on recently revamped state of Michigan assessment tests.

SUCCESSFUL PRACTICES IN LITERACY

In the words of one elementary teacher, the singular focus on literacy became apparent at every turn. Teachers employed best practices. They used their data collectively to determine school wide strategies that targeted student needs. Then they committed to consistently use these strategies. Cross-content literacy practices were used daily in all classes. Additionally staff flexed their innovative muscle to create time for both interventions and enrichments.

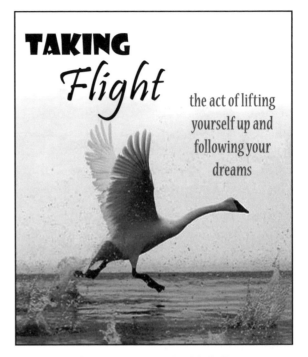

Student Art Work by Molly P.

The staff regarded themselves as literacy learners. They dedicated themselves collectively to grow their instructional expertise around literacy. They committed to consistently use these strategies. There was a stronger link between the written curriculum, the "taught" curriculum, and what was assessed. Consistency of instructional practice, from classroom to classroom and from grade to grade, had become the norm.

Additional efforts included establishment of the literacy coaching network, strengthening of the professional learning communities (PLC) process, continued development of the data warehouse, and greater opportunities for teachers to grow in their literacy practices.

Adult Learning: Develop Structures and Processes for the Learning of All the Adults in the School System

Northview championed collaborative practices through the use of professional learning communities (PLC's), as designed by Richard DuFour (1998). As teachers at all levels met in PLC groups, they used professional conversations that fostered collegiality. One Northview High School teacher commented that they now rely on their colleagues more than they ever have. Through conversations, they share experiences, successes, frustrations, and strategies, and they know they are far more capable together than when they work alone.

Teachers engaged in inquiry and modified instructional strategies informed by their analysis of data. In PLC's, Kathie Lewis, Highlands Middle School literacy coach, had the opportunity to share insights with teachers in her building. She observed that her colleagues are more discriminating about effective strategies. They were able to abandon ineffective methods and irrelevant curriculum standards. As Kathie said, "Through the effort of sharing data and best practice, teachers have the opportunity to better assess the effectiveness of their instruction and make good decisions about what to teach."

RESULTS OF ADULT LEARNING

Northview teachers, through the partnership work, were engaged in their roles in a new way. Traditionally staff looked upon leaders as those in formal roles designated to "make things happen." But in the complexity of today's educational settings administrators cannot, by themselves, know all they need to know. Recognizing staff's knowledge of teaching and learning, the administrative team began to encourage the *development of staff's voice through participation and professional conversations.*

Professional Learning Communities (PLC's)

The format of the professional learning communities gave staff a structure to accomplish its literacy goals. The PLC process was crucial in giving staff the structure, time, and support to come together to work on their instructional practice. Staff collaboration ignited everyone's learning. Teachers assumed responsibility, not only for the learning of assigned students, but for the achievement of their colleagues' students. They came to believe and demonstrate that *"all kids are our kids."*

Staff found a voice not only in PLC meetings but also in curriculum commit-
tees, school improvement leadership, grade level and content meetings, as well
as traditional staff meetings. Gradually administrators welcomed the thinking of
their individual staff members and encouraged them to share their knowledge of
student achievement. This created an emphasis on adult learning for staff and
administrators alike.

A survey assessed improvement in teacher capacity in literacy instruction,
learning, and leading from the beginning to the end of the partnership.

The following are the five areas of highest growth:

- Staff could articulate their responsibility to the district's K-12 mission to
  improve literacy.

- Staff saw themselves as K-12 learners of literacy.

- Staff aligned their instructional practices with the district's K-12 literacy
  focus.

- Staff was provided a variety of methods to acquire information about their
  students.

- Staff was provided opportunities to use data, and ask questions about and
  reflect upon their instructional practice.

To increase the reliability of this research we analyzed staff's comments recorded
during the seven years of the partnership and correlated it to survey results.
Analysis of their comments confirmed what staff had reported on the survey.

A surprising observation was noted at an event for the end-of-partnership
celebration. This was a voluntary work session from 3:45 p.m. to 7:30 p.m. after
a full day of work. In advance we considered a 20% attendance rate positive, yet
over 54% of the Northview staff attended. Staff members had designed the agenda
which included appreciative inquiry and an after-action review. They facilitated
most of the evening's activities, and their questions stimulated conversation about
sustaining this work for the future.

SUCCESSFUL PRACTICES IN ADULT LEARNING

From our survey data, observations, and research, we were able to conclude
the following about adult learning:

- The use of the Learning Cycle model and Professional Conversation formats honored the social nature of learning and supported staff collaboration. Staff participated with peers and administration to share what they knew.

- A process for collaborative learning allowed the staff to make decisions, solve problems, and innovate.

- Given regular data on student learning, staff was able to make increasingly effective instructional decisions.

- Staff felt more powerful when given a voice about the implementation of strategies.

- Staff was willing to assume leadership roles given administrative support and appropriate tools (boundaries, resources, a learning process, quality information, access to one another).

Senge (1990, p. 212) suggests that "an organization's vision grows as a by-product of individual visions and ongoing conversations." In shared leadership, every staff member is enabled to contribute to his peers, administration, and the system. No one's knowledge is unimportant, even the newest teachers. Consider the potential for the system when everyone views himself as a leader, someone who has knowledge to share, and the responsibility to voice it.

As staff increasingly assumed leadership responsibilities, they came to understand:

- They themselves own the knowledge necessary to improve the school system.

- They are responsible to share what they know with one another, administration, and colleagues outside the school system as opportunities arise.

It became obvious that the primary resources for staff's leadership were their *voices* and *participation* through conversation. The interplay of work on adult learning and literacy as well as systems thinking correlated with *an identity of shared leadership for staff.*

Align the School System to Both Student *and* Adult Learning

Northview identified components of the school system which were critical to improving student achievement. Some components were adapted from the Harvard Change Model (Wagner, Kegan, Lahey, Lemons, Garnier, Helsing,

Howell, Thurber Rasmussen, 2006). The components identified in our authentic work include:

- Culture

- Conditions

- Capacity

- Consistency

- Context for change

In order to grow the capacity of the entire system, the administration intentionally nurtured the development of each of these components in support of learning. In combination, these components fostered the learning of all stakeholders and their ability to share what they know. The Board of Education, staff, parent groups, and community stakeholders were engaged in sharing information about student learning. Everyone was called to action and participation. No one was left out.

With administrative support, staff began to design their own learning, debrief results, and make instructional decisions. Staff especially understood that they were expected to be *partners* in improving student achievement and improving instructional practice.

RESULTS OF SYSTEMS THINKING

Staff related the following observations regarding the system:

Culture

- Staff reported a major improvement in the way they worked together to improve student performance. There was a high degree of staff satisfaction and positive morale.

- Principals made collaboration a priority and trusted staff's judgment.

- The administrators expressed appreciation that their staffs were going the extra mile in response to shared high expectations.

- Staff reported that the school system exhibited a healthy, positive, collaborative working environment. People enjoyed working together.

Conditions

- Making time was a huge factor when trying to internalize and plan for a new curricular focus.

- The school system budget was revamped to provide materials and professional development to implement the literacy framework.

- New school improvement goals were focused on literacy strategies and improving student achievement.

- Teachers were able to communicate more effectively with students, parents, and other teachers because they had the information they needed.

Capacity

- Data became a foundation for all decision making.

- Data fostered the improvement of curriculum, instruction, and assessment.

- Data became the key resource in determining what adults needed to learn.

- Staff felt more empowered and involved. Staff opinions mattered.

- Staff made decisions on scheduling and intervention support.

- Staff was asked to give feedback on professional development opportunities and for suggestions for the upcoming year.

Consistency

- In the past four years staff efforts were more focused and systematic. The administration and the staff shared the direction of the school district.

- The Literacy Framework had a huge impact on providing common strategies, vocabulary, and assessments.

- The Instructional Framework established a common vocabulary, practices, and understandings.

Context for Change

- Staff came to understand the dynamics of change.

- Staff used information to improve instructional practice.

- Staff sought information from outside sources that stretched their thinking.

SUCCESSFUL PRACTICES OF SYSTEMS THINKING

The strategies employed in the five components of change, culture, conditions, capacity, and consistency were intentionally aligned to student achievement. The evidence of success in each of these five areas includes:

- *Culture:* Staff relationships improved throughout the system.

- *Context for Change*: Data allowed the system to assess current reality and move toward a common vision. The system understood the change process and it cultivated external partnerships to increase its intellectual resources.

- *Conditions*: The resources and planning for literacy focus were put into place.

- *Capacity:* The use of data allowed the school system to forge a link between student achievement and staff learning. Staff's participation in sharing and creating knowledge promoted learning. Administration's learning leadership fostered a razor sharp focus on literacy, learning, and instruction.

- *Consistency:* Common instructional practices were implemented across the K-12 system. *The vision and mission were shared by all.*

The Northview staff responded with energetic participation in leadership opportunities. Area superintendent Bert Bleke paid the district an interesting compliment. He said, "Northview is quietly becoming the leader in our county and is systematically demonstrating a model of shared leadership and collaboration. They don't make a big deal of it; they just seem to do it naturally. I have observed that the staff is committed to leading the district to be the best it can be. When I talk to Northview teachers, they talk about student learning and their own leadership. That's the way it should be."

"*Invite* everyone's input. *Hear* all voices. *Expect* everyone's participation," became the operational guidelines of the school system.

The story of Orville and Wilbur Wright spanned years of arduous, visionary work. It is a tale of trial and error. Similarly, Northview's story about increasing the learning of *all* resulted in a long, challenging, but most productive FLIGHT! to higher literacy achievement and shared leadership.

• •

• What questions provoke thinking about teaching and learning?

• Why isn't it critical to determine "the best" starting point for school improvement efforts?

• In what ways might data support our improvement efforts at the system, building and classroom levels?

• •

Chapter 2

Packing Our Bag with Expert Knowledge

Tough Questions:

- What do we need to improve our practice?
- Where do we turn for answers?

Key Learning Principles:

- Start anywhere; follow it everywhere (Rogers, 2003-2005).
- Align new learning to the vision.

Main Ideas:

- Data is not only a source of information, but a catalyst for learning.
- We need to integrate the key constructs from notable experts into a coherent whole that can be applied to authentic work.
- The primary work of the school system is teaching and learning.
- Adults in the districts are valued as students of instruction.

*W*hen we travel, we usually plan our itinerary carefully to ensure our expectations are realized. Often we consult a travel agent to help us determine where we want to go and the best ways to get there. Similarly, Northview Public Schools sought outside help in planning its FLIGHT! This assistance came in two forms, a foundation and noted experts in the field of education. Their contributions helped the district increase its capacity in the areas of literacy, adult learning, and systems thinking.

First, Northview forged a partnership with The Ball Foundation. The foundation came with the intention to learn "what works" in improving student literacy. It provided support in the form of thought partnering around literacy. At the outset, this collaborative effort intended to research the benefits of using data to improve instruction. The initial activity of this FLIGHT! quickly became a springboard for learning how to:

- become expert at literacy instruction K-12
- develop structures and processes for adult learning
- align the system to both student and adult learning.

Data became not only a constant source of information but it also shifted learning into high gear for the entire school system. We learned through our work that we can start with a need and let it take us everywhere that follows.

The more data we analyzed, the more we learned. The more we learned, the more capacity we built to understand what we *did not know*, and the more we *needed to know*. This gave rise to our quest for expertise outside our own realm of experience. We sought a research base for our work and studied the writings of a variety of experts.

These experts provided a rationale and tools for developing a K-12 literacy focus. We used their research ideas to understand the importance of adult learning. They guided our thinking in pursuit of our vision. They deepened our knowledge of many disciplines including:

- adult learning
- instruction
- literacy
- leadership
- systems thinking
- data use
- learning organizations

Expert Resources and Influence on Northview Public Schools

Jim Collins	• Focus and Alignment • Flywheel Concept • Hedgehog Concept
David Cooperrider	• Appreciative Inquiry • After Action Review
Richard DuFour Rebecca DuFour Robert Eaker	• Professional Learning Communities • Collaboration • Professional Development • Instructional Interventions
Douglas Fisher	• Literacy Focus • Literacy Framework • Instructional Framework • Shared Literacy Practices
Nancy Frey	• Shared Literacy Practices • Literacy Coaching • Literacy Framework
Michael Fullan Doug Reeves	• Power of Networking • Effective Schools
Ronald Heifitz Marty Linsky	• Adaptive Solutions
Robert Marzano	• Instructional Practices that Work
Robert Marzano Brian McNulty Tim Waters	• Balanced Leadership
Hallie Preskill	• Asset-based Inquiry
Myron Rogers	• Design Teams • Appreciative Inquiry • Communities of Practice • School System Identity • Design Teams • Shared Leadership • Professional Conversations
Michael Schmoker	• School Improvement • Data-Driven Decision Making
Peter Senge	• Systems Thinking • Team Learning • Personal Mastery • Mental Models • Vision and Mission

continued next page

Expert Resources, continued

Tony Wagner Robert Kegan Lisa Lahey Richard W. Lemons Jude Garnier Deborah Helsing Annie Howell Harriette Thurber Rasmussen	• School System Components • Literacy Focus
Deb Wahlstrom	• Data Driven Decision Making
Margaret Wheatley	• Information • Participation • Systems Thinking • Fields of Work <div>Wheatley's quotes are reprinted with permission of publisher. From *Leadership and the New Science* Copyright © 1992 by Margaret Wheatley, Berrett-Koehler Publishers, Inc., San Francisco, CA. All rights reserved. www.bkconnection.com</div>

The reader will encounter a heavy dose of quotes from two of these experts, Margaret Wheatley and Myron Rogers who are occasional partners in consulting and writing. Both have provided rich learning experiences over time for The Ball Foundation. However, it was not until Northview began to wrestle with using the entire system to bolster learning that their teachings began to make sense. Until that time Wheatley's seminal book on systems thinking, *Leadership and the New Science* (1992) collected dust on the shelf. Rogers' ongoing training at the foundation was often met with resistance due to its highly theoretical orientation. Few of us could envision Wheatley and Rogers' concepts applied in the authentic work of education.

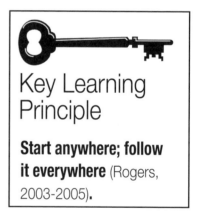

Key Learning Principle

Start anywhere; follow it everywhere (Rogers, 2003-2005)**.**

A student of both Wheatley's and Rogers' thinking, Brayman could spout their assertions but was unable to describe specific examples of their application. However, Wheatley and Rogers' emphasis on interactivity and connectedness, on trust and respect, and on the social nature of learning, resonated with Northview's identity of quality relationships. It appeared to be an optimum time to dust off Wheatley's text and notes from Rogers' training, and blend them into practical learning principles that would guide our work.

In combination Wheatley and Rogers entreat us to rethink our view of leading organizations. They tout the power of collectively identifying our work and its meaning, all continually fed by information. They suggest that once the work is defined, individuals need to be able to connect with one another to mine information together and share what they know. This in itself stimulates learning. Once connected, everyone becomes a learner who is enriched with new information to enhance their professional practice. This provokes change on multiple fronts, necessitating organizational flexibility and nimbleness, the only way a system has a chance of responding to a dynamic environment and maintaining a semblance of health and growth.

Key Learning Principle

New learning must be aligned to the vision.

To these experts, the system itself, by virtue of its dynamic nature, is a treasure trove of resources for supporting learning. However, these resources are not stand-alones to be considered individually. Instead, they are intertwined by virtue of serving the same system and are in relationship with one another through vision, identity, and process.

The most powerful resource in an educational system is its people who can be called upon to meet the needs of the organization based upon their knowledge and ability to share it. By tapping this knowledge, the organization unleashes informal leadership at all levels. People are able to influence the system and each other by providing needed knowledge at the right time and place.

Wheatley talks about these concepts in rich, eloquent language. We often quote her so that the reader can enjoy her own words. Rogers speaks more simply, explaining the powerful concepts in terse phrases that became consistent mantras and key principles throughout our work.

Northview spliced together Wheatley and Rogers' ideas with those of many others listed in the previous chart. No one author's work eclipsed the others. Each was necessary but insufficient in developing our understanding of how to develop a learning organization.

These authors provided the substance for developing a singular, coherent approach to increased learning for all staff and students. As Ester Sternberg, M.D. (2000, p. 204) suggests, "But if we are to make the leap into the next era of [learning], we must also include a look outward from each discipline and a reintegration of them all. For now that the threads have been teased apart and examined individually, it is time to reweave the tapestry and discover how it is woven together. To do this, many gaps must be bridged and many new languages learned."

As Northview staff integrated the new knowledge from these experts, they came to understand that *learning had to be at the center of all their work.* This enabled them to embrace the beliefs that:

- the primary activity throughout the school system is learning to prepare the students, the adults, and the entire school system for the future.
- the adults in the district are valued and see themselves as learners and leaders.
- new learning must be in service to the school system's vision.

Northview staff established an inspiring system-wide vision which was owned by all, "Preparing Students for Life's Next Step." With disciplined intention, they used their data and expert resources to craft a comprehensive plan for progress. Because of their knowledge of change and of how school systems learn, powerful knowledge surfaced that had heretofore not been considered.

It became apparent that collaborative learning is unpredictable; it can take a system almost anywhere. One person's, or one small group's, learning can influence the entire school system and beyond very quickly. This creates a major challenge. How do we integrate and spread this new knowledge for the betterment of students and the entire system?

The vision anchors the rationale for all learning. Using it as a compass we are able to decide what knowledge has value to vision attainment and what does not. It is this *purposeful* alignment of knowledge to the school system's vision that is a hallmark of progress.

• •

• To what professionals can we turn to push our thinking?

• Why is it important to intentionally align professional development with the vision and mission of your system?

• Whose learning is most important: adults' or children's ?

• •

Chapter 3

Orientation to the FLIGHT!
Making This Story Your Own

Tough Question:

- How do we connect new information to what we already know?

Key Learning Principle:

- Be "tight" about what the work is; be "loose" about how it is done.

Main Ideas:

- This text provides a variety of features to engage readers and promote meaning-making.
- The graphic presents key constructs in a visual form which makes the complex simple.
- Tough questions provoke thinking and cause us to look at ourselves and practices.
- The story serves to summarize and model the action necessary to increase student literacy and shared leadership.
- Key Learning Principles guide the processes of the work.

*W*hen we committed to take this FLIGHT!, we anticipated it would enrich our lives in some way. Similarly, to provide readers with a valuable reading experience, we developed multiple features to enhance their engagement and meaning making. The intent is to make the text highly participative and applicable to any school system.

Feature #1: Carry-On

Just like the plastic bag of four-ounce toiletries, we pack essentials into the reader's carry-on at the beginning of each chapter that include tough questions to stretch his thinking, key principles to guide his practice, and main ideas to either reinforce or extend his knowledge. We know that learning is facilitated when the learner has some background knowledge to which he can attach the new. These elements form a consistent framework for each chapter and serve as the chapter summary to carry on—at the beginning of the FLIGHT!

Feature #2: The Graphic

Since the majority of people are visual learners, we developed a graphic to make the story clear and easily understood. It represents the key constructs of 1.) maximizing adult learning; 2.) improving literacy instruction; 3.) using a systems approach. The graphic at the beginning of Part 1 depicts an overview of the entire body of work that led to Northview's system transformation. The graphics found at the beginning of each part of the book provide a visual guide to the contents.

The reader will note that the graphic is a compilation of three areas of work which we call "fields." Typically our profession describes its work in terms of programs, initiatives or mandates; so what is the meaning of fields? This is a concept derived from Wheatley's (1992) work on systems. Brayman, who visited the Northview district only once or twice a week, kept noticing that a small intervention in one place in the district seemed to provoke major changes in other distant parts, or across the entire system. For example, a discussion about an effective literacy practice in one building could affect almost instant application throughout many buildings. Wheatley's field theory provided an explanation for "action at a distance" (Wheatley, 1992, p. 48), that is, for helping us understand how a change could migrate across the organization without some planned intervention.

Fields engage all employees wherever they are in the district. By bringing people together around specified work, fields generate energy and action. When people understand that they are encouraged to share their knowledge and promote new thinking, they come alive. They not only understand their relationship to the district's grand plan, but they see how they can have a direct influence on its accomplishment. This provides a collective and individual sense of purpose.

In Northview the school improvement team was commissioned to increase student achievement and instructional effectiveness. Representatives from each building met at regular intervals to determine the efficacy of the district's instructional effort through the analysis of data at the building and system level. As they met they could see how classroom efforts were connected to the buildings' results, and how the buildings' efforts impacted results across the district. Once they had developed a big picture of the entire system, staff could understand the learning needs of both adults and children and the responsibility the district had to support both. Out of this understanding came the intentional development of two fields of work: adult learning and high quality literacy instruction.

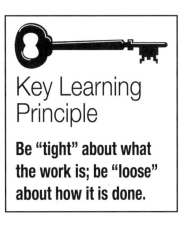

Key Learning Principle

Be "tight" about what the work is; be "loose" about how it is done.

The connectivity within and across fields creates a context for "leaps of understanding" and change to take place. This interconnectedness can eliminate the need for a step-by-step, totally sequential transfer of information, learning and action. Jumps in understanding and changes in behavior materialize unpredictably out of thin air. The progress we had planned for in increments seems to erupt spontaneously, often rendering our carefully laid plans obsolete. We scratch our heads wondering if there *is* any such thing as control.

Although a field itself is invisible, its influence is visible. Wheatley (1992) suggests that because we cannot detect fields through our senses, they are non-material. However, they are very real. Wheatley (1992) compares them to an ocean with invisible influences and structures that connect. For example, while we cannot see leadership, we still see its effects.

There are innumerable fields in any system. For our purposes we call out three fields which blend into a simple picture of a school system. Singly they serve little purpose. Together they create a picture of a whole system that exists to foster student achievement. The fields that we call out (next page) are: high quality literacy instruction, adult learning and systems work. The work in each of these fields is inextricably interrelated. Everyone in the district is influenced by all of them and has the opportunity to impact each of them through their learning, and knowledge sharing. As you look at the graphics (pp. 28-29), picture these fields awash with district stakeholders, solutions, challenges, and choices. Visualize formal and informal connections between the stakeholders in each field. Imagine everyone in each field as a learner, sharing what they know and creating new skills and knowledge. All this can happen when staff is bound together in a common effort.

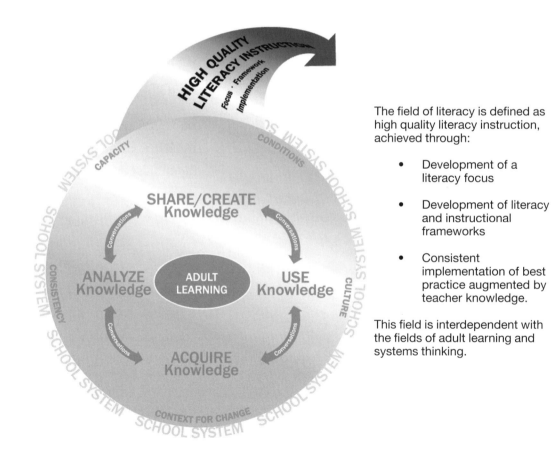

The field of literacy is defined as high quality literacy instruction, achieved through:

- Development of a literacy focus

- Development of literacy and instructional frameworks

- Consistent implementation of best practice augmented by teacher knowledge.

This field is interdependent with the fields of adult learning and systems thinking.

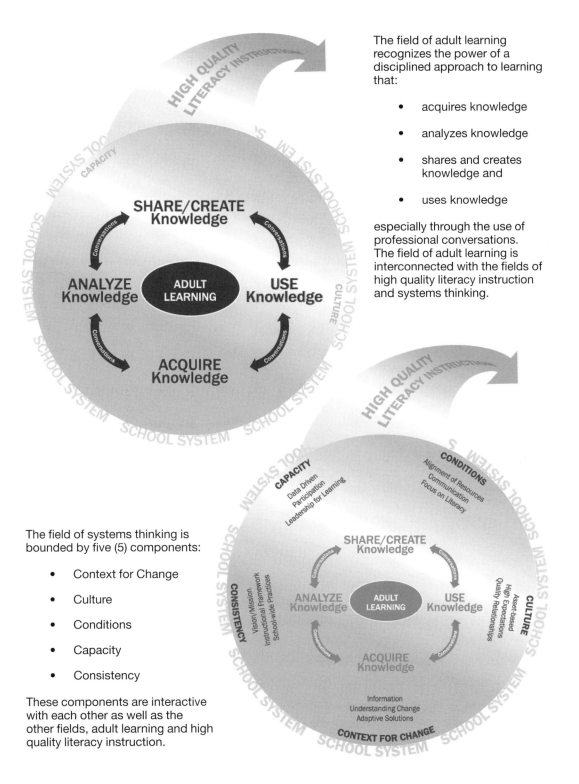

The field of adult learning recognizes the power of a disciplined approach to learning that:

- acquires knowledge
- analyzes knowledge
- shares and creates knowledge and
- uses knowledge

especially through the use of professional conversations. The field of adult learning is interconnected with the fields of high quality literacy instruction and systems thinking.

The field of systems thinking is bounded by five (5) components:

- Context for Change
- Culture
- Conditions
- Capacity
- Consistency

These components are interactive with each other as well as the other fields, adult learning and high quality literacy instruction.

Staff Conversations

The Three Authors' Conversation:

It's Really Doable

When Jacqueline Brayman presented the draft of this graphic to her fellow authors, they responded, "It makes the complex, simple. We now can actually connect facets of our work that used to be disconnected. The graphic promotes a consistent vocabulary so we can all speak the same language. All of a sudden the huge challenge of improving student achievement seems doable instead of daunting. And we do not all have to do it all at once. What a relief!"

Feature #3: The Story

We chose the story form for this book because for most of us the stories of our professional lives flow from our personal missions of "wanting to make a difference." Day in and out we work tirelessly in the hopes that what we do will improve the lives of others and leave the world a better place. It is a story line that never reaches climax—we are in a profession where the work is never done.

From the onset of spoken language, six of the most impactful words in history have been, "Let me tell you a story." According to Ryan Matthews (2008, p. 24), futurist and corporate storyteller, "Throughout humanity's time on earth, stories have been the universal, and a preferred way of passing down history, culture, tradition, wisdom, and meaning. They also have been used to give meaning to individual lives, family structure, societies and even civilizations." Matthews explains that stories serve many functions including:

- defining a group's identity
- simplifying complex issues
- illustrating relationships
- summarizing complex history
- transferring and preserving core values
- modeling behavior
- providing detailed paths to [a better future].

In combination, these functions facilitate our attempt to connect with and make meaning for the reader.

The work in Northview is far more than a series of documented planned activities. It is the combination of hundreds of stories that took place in the classroom, in the school buildings, and across the district, connecting one to another over time. None of these individual tales was critical to Northview's transformative effort to improve student achievement. Instead it is the relationship of all of the stories to one another and to the vision of the district that binds them together in a coherent whole and gives meaning to Northview's "plot."

As story after story emerged, the Northview staff began to see themselves in each other's story. They developed the ability to listen to different interpretations of information and process them with a common purpose. What evolved over time was the *clarity* of the Northview story. Eventually the staff came to realize their individual and collective responsibility to learn.

It is impossible to tell the story of a school system's transformation in a linear, sequential fashion. When everyone is a learner, the system abounds with information, learning and action. There are no identifiable milestones. Instead, the growth of capacity of each individual and the system tells the story. This growth occurs in the three fields of work which are separate conceptually, but connected dynamically in authentic work. The reader will note occasional overlap of parts of this book because all of the people and all of the fields of work are interconnected through their relationships, learning, and practice.

Feature #4: Staff Conversations

As part of the ongoing story, we captured staff's musings about their own learning. The intent is for the reader to see themselves reflected in staff's insights. According to Wagner and Kegan, ". . .hearing the stories, hopes and opinions of those in our own community moves us emotionally, reminds us of the moral imperative behind our work, and enables us to see the information as living in three dimensions instead of in just one. The stories, the faces, and the voices remain with us with insistency that numbers can rarely inspire" (Wagner, Kegan, Lahey, Lemons, Garnier, Helsing, Howell, & Thurber Rasmussen, 2006, p. 135).

Staff Conversations

Staff conversations will appear in the text in this way:

Feature #5: Key Learning Principles

From theory and research we extracted a set of guiding principles for our efforts, simple ideas from complex information. We called out these principles regularly to help us stay the course. While a vision and mission provided guidance for decisions about content of the work, these "Key Learning Principles" gave us a rationale for the processes we employed. These principles are highlighted in the text as shown at right:

Key Learning Principle

Feature #6: Tough Questions

Our thought partners, The Ball Foundation, continually fed information back to us about ourselves by holding up a figurative mirror. This required us to thicken our skin. Their favorite phrases seemed to be:

- And now I'm going to push on your thinking. . . .

- How does that relate to the mission and vision?

- What does this mean to instructional practice?

- What assumptions might you be operating from?

- What does your data tell you about student learning?

- What assets are available from which to springboard?

- What has worked in the past?

- Who should be involved in this effort due to their ability to share it with others?

Northview had to learn to process the foundation's input from a purely objective level rather than from our hearts to prevent defensiveness. That did not keep us, both district and foundation staff, from getting angry and having testy, lively conversations. We learned that the differences between the two organizations' perspectives stimulated much learning for both.

When we remembered that the foundation had no motive other than our success, we could relax with their provocation and figure out, "What does this mean to us and how can we use it to grow?" Our foundation representative, Brayman, challenged our thinking about ourselves, our policies, and our practices with "Tough Questions."

The questions: • challenged assumptions
                 • generated energy
                 • stimulated reflection
                 • and evoked deeper meaning.

The most important result of these interactions was that *staff began to ask tough questions of themselves*. Tough questions will be posed at the beginning of each chapter in the Carry-On.

Feature #7: Student Graphic Designs

Northview High School's art students create unique graphically designed posters. Unlike most art that students produce, these graphic posters have the express purpose of assisting fellow students in learning key vocabulary words, termed, "*Words of the Week.*" The posters are a public affirmation and creative expression of the importance of literacy at the school. They are a connection that the art teachers make to the district's literacy goals. They demonstrate the priority teachers place on vocabulary development, one of Northview High School's designated school-wide literacy strategies.

Taking Flight to Literacy and Leadership! is brimming with important terms related to building the capacity of school systems to learn and grow. We provided Northview High School art students a list of approximately twenty of these terms. We invited them to design a graphic illustrating what the word *meant to them*. The book features many of the designs created by students to enhance the readers' understanding of these concepts.

These graphic designs are highlighted in the text as:

Student Art Work by

Feature #8: "Take-Aways"

At the end of every FLIGHT! we can often catch a glimpse of our captain and co-pilot checking their gauges and completing paperwork before they disembark. They are processing the results of their own work. Similarly at the end of each chapter is a suitcase for "Take-Aways." It is for the reader to fill with new understandings and applications for his own work. Questions are provided to provoke the reader to consider "What does this mean to me? How might I use it to strengthen the good things I am already doing?"

As every school practitioner knows, the work of improving schools and student achievement is extraordinarily complex. One can become immobilized by the sheer magnitude of the responsibility. However, the story of Northview Public Schools is proof that it can be done—when everyone in the district is involved—*everyone,* with no exceptions.

No matter where you sit in your district, all the concepts in this book apply. And so, Ladies and Gentlemen, welcome aboard. Fasten your seatbelts and prepare for your learning journey. Let's take FLIGHT!

• •

• How can we make our work both "loose" and "tight" at the same time?

• What is the value of using stories as a tool in our work?

• What key learning principles do we use as a mantra with our own staff? What is their importance?

• •

PART 2:
FLIGHT! to Literacy

To improve the achievement of each individual student, Northview developed a district-wide literacy focus.

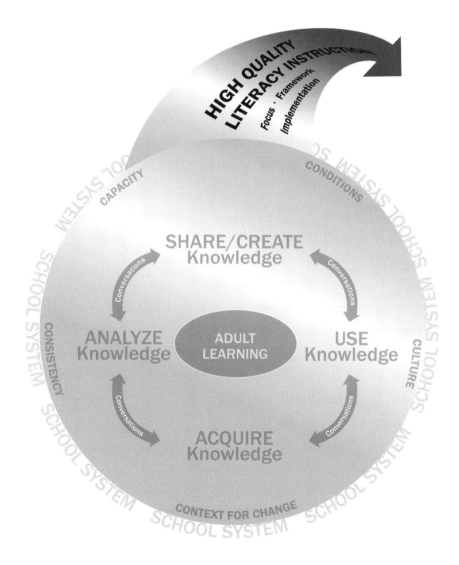

Chapter 4

Each and Every vs. All

Tough Questions:

- How do we determine if students already know what we intend to teach?

- How will we know if each student is learning?

- What will we do when some students do not learn?

- What will we do to enrich student learning?
  (DuFour, DuFour, Eaker, 2008)

Key Learning Principle:

- Success is measured one student at a time.

Main Ideas:

- No Child Left Behind Act of 2001 emphasizes the achievement of each student which shifts the target for success from groups to every single student.

- Professional Learning Communities provoke the need for achievement data.

" *M* ore than forty million adults in the United States lack the basic reading skills to fill out a job application or read a child's book. Many new immigrants to our country cannot speak English well enough to assimilate successfully into the American way of life.

This inability to verbally communicate with others, to read simple directions, road signs and addresses or even a restaurant menu, often causes major obstacles in social and career interactions and severely limits the quality of life" (Literacy Council of Upper Pinellas County, Inc., 2009, p. 1).

The No Child Left Behind Act of 2001 (NCLB) is an attempt by the federal government to eradicate these worrisome statistics through proactive measures in our public school systems. NCLB is a reauthorization of the Elementary and Secondary Education Act (ESEA), the basic federal law in pre-collegiate education. ESEA, and now NCLB, are the government's program for aiding the disadvantaged (Title I) and English-language learners (Title III). NCLB has become the federal government's primary education policy. It has set standards that impact every public school in America. Its intent is to employ measures to improve achievement and accountability so that all schools make "adequate yearly progress" in student achievement and employ teachers who are "highly qualified."

No Child Left Behind breaks tradition with measuring the progress of groups of students, traditionally defined by grade level. NCLB ramps up levels of account-ability by requiring the measurement of ethnic groups' and *each and every child's achievement*. Under NCLB every student is to be proficient in reading, writing, and mathematics skills by 2014 as measured by state determined assessments. NCLB requires all states to measure adequate yearly progress of individuals, subgroups, and entire grades and buildings. Data disaggregation makes evident areas of profi-ciency and concern for all those assessed, with the emphasis on the performance of *each* individual student.

To make meaning of assessment results, teachers have to have a certain level of skill with data. Northview's Director of Instruction, Grey, and district assess-ment experts went building to building to teach data analysis skills to staff. *Once Northview teachers had specific data skills at their disposal, they embraced the task of regularly analyzing the progress of individual students in order to guide their day-to-day instruction.*

They began to exercise their growing skill in developing questions about teaching and learning:

- Is every student learning?

- Is our instruction effective?

- What successful strategies should we build upon and share?

- What should we do differently to achieve greater results?

- Will this prepare students for the demands of the 21st century?

Teachers were feeling pressure from both internal and external sources to answer these questions. Not only was the federal government demanding that *each* student achieve success, differences in district students' skill abilities were widening. Staff was challenged by the powerful questions of the Professional Learning Communities (PLC) model (DuFour, DuFour, Eaker, Karhanek, 2004):

1. What do we want students to learn?

2. How do we know each student is learning?

3. What happens when a student does not learn?

Northview adopted the Professional Learning Communities (PLC) concept in an attempt to answer these critical questions. The collaborative structure of the PLC's created a forum to utilize data in professional conversations about the achievement of individuals and groups of students. The more teachers examined data in their PLC groups, the more data they requested concerning each student's achievement. They valued the availability on their desktops of each student's achievement data.

When staff tackled the first PLC question, "What do we want students to learn?" they were really considering

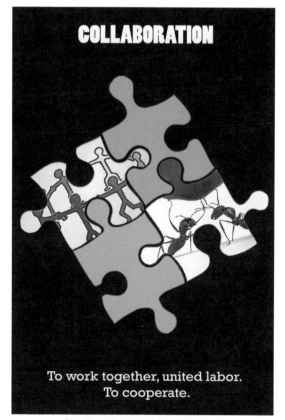

COLLABORATION

To work together, united labor.
To cooperate.

Student Art Work by Katelyn F.

a broader question, now currently stated in the Professional Learning Communities' model as, "How do we know students have acquired the intended knowledge, skills, and dispositions of this course, grade level, or unit of instruction?" (DuFour, DuFour, Eaker, 2008, p.184).

This was a time of analysis in Northview. Teachers held conversations about curriculum mapping and alignment. They wrestled with issues of common assessments, standards, benchmarks, and length of time for instruction. They wondered, "What is most important? What do we need to consider? How will we know if students are learning? What is intended and what might we need to create to give us better information?

DuFour refers to the "power of formative assessments, assessments used as part of the teaching and learning process instead of assessments administered only to provide a grade" (p. 26). Teachers grew in their expertise using formative and common assessments to monitor each and every student's progress. This took a great deal of time and effort but produced positive results when teachers could better shine a light on just exactly what students needed in their learning. It allowed them to "drill down" and consequently better tailor interventions and enrichments for students.

The second PLC question, "How do we know each student is learning?" has been tweaked to state, "How will we know if each student is learning each of the essential skills, concepts, and dispositions we have deemed most essential?" DuFour states, "This question serves as the linchpin of the (PLC) collaborative team process." Further he states, "Thus, the work of the collaborative team flows up and down from the challenge of assessing student learning in the most authentic and beneficial ways" (p. 186).

In Northview the challenge of assessing student learning opened up deep conversations about:

- academic expectations
- grading practices
- first time instruction
- reteaching opportunities
- teacher expectations and more.

The third PLC question, "What happens in our school when a student does not learn?" has expanded into, "How will we respond when some of our students do not learn? What process will we put in place to ensure students receive additional time and support for learning in a timely, directive, and systematic way?" (p. 187). DuFour suggests, "We submit that what typically happens when a student does not learn will depend on the practices of his or her individual teacher rather than on any coordinated, collective response."

Key Learning Principle

Success is measured one student at a time.

Northview conducted an internal assessment at every building to determine available interventions. Principals were responsible to flesh out what interventions were occurring building-wide and district-wide. These were some of the questions staff asked of themselves:

- What interventions do we offer now?

- How do teachers partner to differentiate interventions for students? (example: all math teachers plan differentiated interventions)

- Is there a "building-wide" response to interventions?

- How can we utilize all available adults in the building, though they may not have the student in class, such as the building principal, guidance counselors, social workers, art, physical education, music and technology teachers and train them to conduct intervention lessons for students one-on-one or in small groups?

- How can we creatively offer interventions before school, after school, during lunch or student seminar time (at the high school level) and what would we need to plan to make that happen?

- How can we get support from the district office to offer transportation for students wishing to stay later than the regularly scheduled bus routes and coordinate that district-wide?

- How can we engage parents, school volunteers, and the community in some way?

- Based upon data, what could we design to provide more effective interventions?

At the time, teachers had not considered, nor had the PLC model included, the fourth PLC question that was later added. That question was, "How will we enrich and extend the learning for students who are already proficient?" (p.187) When we say Northview teachers did not initially consider this question, they actually could not avoid it. Of course, there would be students who already demonstrated proficiency and needed extended learning opportunities. Thus, born out of a new attention to each and every student's progress, and the analysis of what interventions were in place at the building level, teachers now planned for differentiation in terms of both intervention and enrichment.

As a result of broad participation and a great deal of creative planning, every school redesigned their schedules. Schools determined how to offer a 30-minute daily period that did not conflict with regular classroom instruction. It was additional. Some schools captured time during what used to be a "homeroom period" of sorts for elementary students. One middle school enacted the 30-minute daily intervention/enrichment period. Another set up before and after school times and various teachers agreed to provide interventions. Any student needing help was welcome to attend. At the high school, seminar time was carved out of the day and held sacred to ensure support for students. This was the ideal time for a student to obtain additional interventions as well as extended learning opportunities.

Student achievement data became central to school improvement meetings, staff meetings, child studies, and grade level PLC's. As teachers became more astute in their use of data, they understood fully who was learning and who was not. This growing expertise was accompanied by a gnawing realization that "We can do better." State assessments along with school system data confirmed that students, *each and every one*, could be achieving at higher levels. Now, the system had the data, the time, and the structures to respond to each student's needs.

Staff Conversations

A Conversation with Mary Lou Ohnsmann, Teacher:

Data Informs My Instruction

At the building and classroom levels data began to influence instructional planning. Still teachers wondered what opportunities existed at the district level to ramp up the quality of instruction for each student.

One West Oakview fourth grade teacher, Mary Lou Ohnsmann, comments, "Understanding and making ,

"Understanding and making adaptations and changes in our PLC grade level work has occurred over the course of the year. Coupled with district support, we have refocused our time and centered conversations on the data we have received. As each of my students' literacy scores were broken down, I immediately recognized what needed to change. I refocused my goals in writing. I had specific data that informed my teaching, and I used it to help my students make greater connections."

Just like airlines hold to the standard that each and every flight is a safe one, so too, do school systems need to ensure the success of *each* and *every* student.

• **What is the power of DuFour, DuFour, Eaker and Kahanek's four (4) questions?**

• **How do these questions influence our professional practice?**

• **How do these questions impact our desire to "make a difference" through our professional work?**

Chapter 5

The Power of a Singular Focus:
Literacy

Tough Questions:

- What is the power of an instructional focus?

- How do you determine it?

Key Learning Principle:

- Develop a Focus!

Main Ideas:

- When teachers use data to plan instruction, they are better able to meet the needs of students.

- An instructional focus leads all other instructional work.

- By making literacy our primary focus, we contribute to the success of each student in all content areas.

*W*hen teachers began to use their data on a daily basis to plan their instruction and assessment, they found they were better able to meet the needs of their students. By studying research Northview staff concluded that:

- success in every content area is dependent upon strong literacy skills.

- reading ability contributes 80-90% to their success in social studies, writing, and language arts.

- reading ability contributes 60-70% to their success in math.

- reading ability contributes 70-80% to their success in science.

It became obvious that the element common to every content area was literacy. It was the unifying bond between subjects and grade levels. Strong literacy skills were essential for student success in every aspect of the K-12 experience and beyond.

Tony Wagner, in *Making the Grade* (2003, p. 142) suggests that "One of the great mistakes of the high-stakes testing movement in my judgment is the attempt to test an ever-increasing number of subject areas as if they all mattered equally. High-level math skills are—foolishly, I think—a requirement for college, but how often are they used by adults in everyday life? By contrast, a high level of literacy—the ability to comprehend complex material, synthesize information, and present it clearly, both orally and in writing—is an indispensable skill in most workplaces today."

In *Results Now: How We Can Achieve Unprecedented Improvements in Teaching and Learning* (2006, p. 57), Michael Schmoker stresses, "The gateway to a good education is literacy." He further states, "Literacy is pivotal to acquiring the type of education that is the path to economic and political power."

A data-driven collaborative culture was developing as Northview teachers began sharing results and best literacy practices. "Through the professional learning communities' use of data, teachers benefit from sharing and learning literacy strategies that affect their students. It's all about results, and data tell the story," commented one principal, Cindi O'Connor.

Repeatedly, teachers were echoing the need for common, consistent literacy goals, K-12 because of insights gleaned from data. As conversations about literacy took place between classrooms, departments, and across building boundaries, the need for relevant meaningful data continued to grow as did requests for a coherent district focus on literacy. Student achievement results varied between buildings and even from classroom to classroom. Calls now came from teachers as well as administrators for maximizing instructional effectiveness with a common focus on literacy.

Because of its critical importance to every aspect of the curriculum, we strongly believed a singular focus on literacy would deliver the most significant results. In *The Power of Focus*, authors Nelson, Palumbo, Cudiero, and Leight (2005) state that having one specific academic area of the curriculum chosen by staff on which to focus is the highest priority for school improvement. They admonish educators that this instructional focus must come first and drives all other instructional work. In their words, ". . .we have discovered that one key to high performing or rapidly improving schools is they have found a way to focus their efforts and not try to do everything all at once. These schools have learned to be proactive and to focus on *one* specific instructional area of the curriculum—an area that they consider to be the most important for their students to know and be able to do to be successful in life" (p. 20).

Leadership's Role in Developing a Focus

Administrative retreats were powerful opportunities for Northview's administrators to come together in their own professional learning community. Retreats were held two to three times a year at an off-site location in close proximity to the district, for purposes of planning and collaborating. Superintendent Stearns believed, "Administrators need an environment where they can grow their administrative skills before they publicly are called upon to apply them. What we were after was giving them an opportunity to build some expertise and confidence in their own leadership skills and abilities."

Brayman, our Ball Foundation representative, adds, "There is great value in these opportunities. Administrators can "push-back" on each other's thinking, clarify their understandings, and come to common agreements. It gets people to sift through their own set of assumptions and their own meanings and come to a *common* meaning. They determine what they can support and what they can believe in together."

One particular retreat stands out as especially significant. The retreat of the Northview Administra-

Key Learning Principle

Develop a Focus!
(Nelson, Palumbo, Cudeiro, and Leight, 2005)

tive Team (Ad Team) of February 6, 2006, promised to be a day of great learning.

The retreat was planned in the usual way. Several members of the administrative team met for a process called a "design team" to plan the retreat on behalf of their colleagues. The responsibility to serve on a design team rotated with all the administrators.

For this retreat, administrators knew that the goal of the Superintendent, Board of Education, administrators, and staff was to develop a district instructional focus. It was agreed that the final decision for selecting the focus would only be made after additional input from staff.

Prior to the retreat, administrators were asked to:

- Read selected articles on the importance of focus.

- Bring their school's achievement data and main areas of strengths and needs (compiled with their school improvement team).

- Complete a staff survey to determine instructional practices currently in use and desired practices for the future.

- Hold conversations with their School Improvement Team regarding establishing a district-wide focus and their recommendations for it.

During the actual retreat administrators explained graphics to their colleagues of their building's achievement and survey data, along with staff recommendations. There was open communication as administrators asked questions to build cross-district understandings.

The Superintendent and Brayman asked administrators to engage in a "gallery walk." A gallery walk is simply a way to view graphically-represented material by walking along past it. Directions for the administrative gallery walk included:

- Attend to the goal of identifying a district-wide focus that will impact student achievement and one that staff can rally around.

- Reflect upon, analyze, and draw assumptions about the data and comments individually, at first.

- Repeat the process with a partner. Include a conversation about the strengths and needs that all buildings have in common.

- As a group, identify a focus that will give us the greatest "educational bang for the buck . . . for our collective efforts." It should build upon strengths while intentionally addressing the areas of need.

Stearns and Brayman led the group in a debrief. Overwhelmingly the group targeted literacy as the *one collective focus* that would result in the greatest impact on student achievement across the grades and buildings. The data had clearly shown the need. Staff comments expressed a desire to focus district efforts in a way that would maximize their instructional efforts.

Administrators experienced a great "Aha" in their conversations. A logic around literacy developed and the thinking sounded something like this: "If we make literacy our primary work, we are contributing to the success of each and every student in *all* content areas, equipping them for the workplace, and enabling them to make quality decisions for their future citizenship and personal lives. By defining our common work as literacy throughout the district, we create the opportunity for increased success, not only for each student, but also for staff."

Collectively administrators came to common agreements about taking this message back to staff. A discussion was held on leadership skills that would be needed to lead the literacy focus. Would the leaders themselves be responsible for knowing everything about literacy? How would this impact what we do with students, professional development efforts, staff meetings, instructional time, budgets, stakeholder involvement, and who would support administrators in this work? It was agreed that administrators would not be responsible for knowing every single reading or writing strategy; however, they should be familiar with them. The more important focus of their leadership now would focus on en-

Focus
A central point, as of attraction, attention, or activity.

Student Art Work by John R.

suring that students were learning and that teachers were using best practices. They committed to work collaboratively and consistently. They would rely upon each other for support as they ventured forward.

Staff Conversations

A Conversation with Jenny Barnes, Elementary Teacher:

Focus Brings Effective Instruction

In the words of one elementary teacher, Jenny Barnes, "I felt energized when we met as a district to discuss the meaning of our entire PLC work—now focused on literacy. I believe that, as a district, we are moving forward toward each and every student's greater good. We are functioning more efficiently and effectively to make better use of our instructional time and are guiding our colleagues toward better learning around literacy."

Until Northview determined a focus, instructional priorities remained elusive. What was there to rally around, to unify all the effort? Whether teachers' responsibility was for twenty-eight or one-hundred fifty students a day, how should they best think about serving their students well? The identified instructional focus of literacy gave teachers a place to start together and a map to follow.

One high school colleague echoed these sentiments, "Keep the literacy focus; it has become the driving force in Northview. This united effort helps the entire system and makes the mission of educating each student come alive. Through the focus on literacy, we see the link between teaching and student achievement. It is clear and *we all know the common goal.*"

• **What instructional focus might have the biggest impact on our students' achievement?**

• **Tony Wagner suggests that the school district that has 10 goals, has no goals (2006). What did he mean?**

• **How might an instructional focus positively influence a school system's efficiency and effectiveness?**

Chapter 6

Developing the Literacy Framework

Tough Question:

- How do we develop a common understanding of our practice?

Key Learning Principle:

- Sharing a common understanding of our practice builds capacity.

Main Ideas:

- A common definition, vocabulary, and strategies for literacy are critical for staff to be able to share their expertise.

- Establishment of a literacy framework fosters consistency in practice.

- Participation of staff in the creation of a literacy framework engenders ownership and sustainability.

*B*efore any literacy work could be accomplished with the entire K-12 staff, ground work had to be laid. The challenge was figuring out exactly where to start.

For years Northview had a district Language Arts Committee. Because the work to lead literacy initiatives now needed to engage all content areas, not just the language arts, it was important that literacy leadership reflected a broader view. Thus, a subcommittee was formed that came to be regarded as a Literacy Leadership Group. All buildings had representatives from various content areas and departments that served on the Literacy Leadership Group.

As a razor-sharp focus on literacy evolved, an interesting assumption surfaced. Teachers had assumed they could clearly articulate what literacy was and what it meant. But surprisingly, even teachers within the same grade level defined it differently and used different vernacular for literacy terms.

Then-Director of Instruction Grey commented in her work with the literacy team, "It is evident that teachers cannot work to improve something that they don't totally understand nor have common understandings of. Certainly staff cannot hope to have K-12 conversations around literacy until they first define it, discuss it, and come to common agreements."

Conducting an Audit on Literacy Instructional Practices

The Northview Literacy Leadership Group engaged in conversations to analyze existing practices. The district called upon an external friend and literacy leader, Char Firlik. She conducted an activity that helped staff recognize their inconsistencies. She introduced vocabulary from the state and local standards in the language arts strands of reading, writing, speaking, listening, viewing, and research. Each person referenced the language arts vocabulary for their grade level and circled words that they taught but for which they used a different term.

For example, if a curriculum standard required students to "edit" as a writing revision strategy, one classroom teacher may call the process, "double check," while another may call it a "repeat and review." Or if students were to engage in the process called "brainstorming" as a prewriting strategy, one teacher may label it as a "quick think," while another teacher might refer to it as a "brain burst." Teachers graphed and charted words about literacy within and then across the grade levels and noted the variety of vocabulary used. It was of special note that in *all* cases, teachers said although they used different terms, they *were* teaching the same concept.

Staff Conversations

A Conversation with Tammy Cannon, First Grade Teacher, and Kathy Vogel, Seventh Grade Teacher:

We Need Consistency

"We were literally all over the board," said a first grade teacher, Tammy Cannon. A seventh grade teacher, Kathy Vogel added, "It was such an eye-opener to see that we were using our own individual literacy language with our students. As students move from grade to grade we wanted to make sure there was no confusion in the teaching and testing vocabulary that teachers use. We wanted to achieve some consistency."

One thing became crystal clear to staff: defining literacy was a critical need with implications for every grade level. Research supported development of a "literacy framework" and teachers speculated that this could provide a structure for instructional improvement throughout the district. A literacy framework expresses a school system's beliefs and commitments about literacy learning. It is meant to facilitate common understandings and language about literacy. When a district holds a common knowledge base about quality literacy instruction, educators are able to share their literacy expertise with peers and create improved instruction. A framework also provides a defined field of best practices for professional learning.

"A literacy-based school stresses the unity of learning through language. It looks at how children learn and how teaching practices affect the learning" (Booth, Rowsell, 2002, p. 61). ". . . All of the successful schools we have observed have in common a strong curriculum and instruction focus, centered around good literacy initiatives and strong assessment programs" (p. 32).

Northview believed that a literacy framework would solidify and articulate its common understandings and practices around literacy. They wanted to share consistent research-based literacy instruction. As Amy Goodman (2005, p. 12) writes, "With a plethora of strategies from which to choose, teachers (in our school) were overwhelmed and inefficient, causing instruction to become hit or miss. From class to class there was little consistency or curriculum alignment. It became apparent that strategy instruction needed to be organized in such a way that it became the norm and not the exception. Students deserve explicit, sequenced instruction from all of their teachers in a meaningful, connected way."

Motivated by reading about the benefits of a consistent literacy framework, the school system's literacy leadership group began the development process with two questions: What is literacy? What are our expectations of student learning and instruction that should be communicated in a framework? The group determined both a process and content for this work.

Student Art Work by Dana C.

The *process* to develop the literacy framework included:

- inviting all interested colleagues into the work
- gathering input from fellow teachers who were not formally involved
- holding book studies to deepen literacy expertise
- hosting feedback sessions to check for staff's understanding
- forging critical friendships with area experts.

The *content* of the literacy framework was comprised of:

- a definition of literacy
- a set of core values and beliefs about literacy
- research-based literacy practices
- an instructional framework that sets a standard for quality practice.

Northview adopted the definition of literacy as follows:

"Literacy is defined as the continual process of constructing meaning through listening, speaking, reading, writing, and interacting with people and their environment" (Kent Intermediate School District, 2006).

The following is the framework developed by the Northview Literacy Leadership Group, in consultation with staff:

NORTHVIEW PUBLIC SCHOOLS K-12 LITERACY FRAMEWORK
(Northview adaptation based upon original by Douglas Fisher and Nancy Frey.)

The Core Instructional Components

	Reading	Writing	Oral Language
CORE INSTRUCTIONAL COMPONENTS Developed using _Professional Learning Communities_ **MI Standards based at appropriate level of thinking** **Using many varieties and levels of reading material** **With many opportunities for student choice and conversation** **In all content areas**	• Word Study (phonemic awareness, phonics, vocabulary, spelling) • Cueing systems (graphophonic, semantic, syntactic, pragmatic) • Comprehension strategies (monitoring and clarifying, making connections, questioning, visualizing, inferring, determining importance, synthesizing) • Metacognitive strategies • Text structure skills (fiction & non-fiction)	• Writing processes • _6+1 Traits_ (ideas, organization, voice, sentence fluency, word choice, conventions, presentation) • Vocabulary study of roots, prefixes and suffixes • Form and function of genres • Meaningful and authentic research • Power writing (fluency building) • John Collins' 5 types of writing • Writing Workshop (Lucy Calkins Writing Kits)	• Substantive conversations about reading and writing daily • Accountable talk (questioning, elaborating, extending, evaluating) • Active and reflective listening • Language registers (informal and formal) • Prosody (expression) • Public speaking skills

Instructional Framework for Gradual Release of Responsibility

Direct Instruction/ Modeling (daily focus lessons)	• Read alouds • Shared reading • Think alouds • Text coding • Read-Write-Talk	• Write alouds • Shared writing • Language Experience Approach • Interactive writing • Cornell notemaking and notetaking • Power writing	• Storytelling • Think-pair-share • Read-Write-Talk • KWL charts
Guided Instruction (flexible and non permanent grouping)	• Guided reading • Comprehension strategies • Responding to text • Conferencing • Intervention	• Guided Writing • Writing models • Conferencing • Intervention	• Discussion groups • Presentation skills • Oral cloze
Collaborative Learning	• Literature circles • Book clubs • Reciprocal teaching • Partner reading • Word study station • Content reading station	• Progressive writing • Paired writing • Group composition • Author's chair • Peer response to writing • Content writing station	• Listening stations • Group retelling • Critical thinking discussions • Cooperative learning • Reader's theatre
Independent Practice with Conferring (a powerful practice for making individual contact with each child)	• Reading for pleasure and lifelong learning • Independent reading • Sustained silent reading • Notemaking • Participation in reading conferences	• Daily writing as a response to reading and learning • Daily writing (e.g., journals, essays, short stories, poetry, etc.) • Writing to learn • RAFT writing • Participation in writing conferences	• Following directions • Presentation practice • Listening stations • Cornell notetaking
Assessment	• Common assessments (formative & summative) • Developmental Reading Assessment (D.R.A.) • MLPP • Running records • Gates MacGinitie Test • Scholastic Reading Counts • MEAP state test • Scholastic Reading Inventory (S.R.I.) • Reading fluency and endurance • Informal Reading Inventories • Self assessments	• Common assessments (formative and summative) • Grade level writing prompts • District/state holistic writing rubrics • District/classroom analytic rubrics • MEAP state assessment • Writing fluency and endurance • K-8 Portfolio • Self assessments	• Common assessments (formative and summative) • Speaking checklist/ rubrics • Listening checklist/ rubric • Self assessments

One source for inspiration for Northview's literacy framework came from the success story of a nationally acclaimed literacy expert, Doug Fisher. Fisher attributed his success at Hoover High School in San Diego, California, to having a concise literacy focus. He worked with staff to develop a literacy framework and school wide literacy practices. Hoover employed consistent literacy strategies, hit their state assessment targets, and the "school's students' average reading level, as measured by the Gates-MacGinitie Reading Test, rose over a four year period from 4.3 to 7.2" (Ivey and Fisher, 2005, p. 9).

At Hoover High, the school's achievement levels had been some of the lowest in all of California. After development of a literacy framework, everyone could clearly understand the literacy plan; it became the basis of their professional development and at the heart of the building's professional conversations. Fisher shared that it is essential that staff is part of the process. At Hoover High he says, "Shared decisions of the staff development committee and school governance helped us articulate a school wide focus on instruction. Subsequent professional development has built the teachers' ability to implement each (literacy) practice" (Fisher, Frey, Williams, 2002, p. 73).

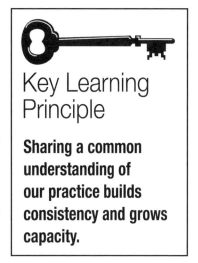

Key Learning Principle

Sharing a common understanding of our practice builds consistency and grows capacity.

The value of having everyone "on the same page and understanding the literacy focus" is that students benefit. With the literacy focus, students can concentrate on content rather than relearning strategies that change from teacher to teacher, classroom to classroom, and grade to grade. Gains in achievement can be accomplished when the school has a consistent, clear, simple literacy focus. For Northview, Fisher's story was an encouraging model of what could happen when the district made literacy its *first priority.*

Following Fisher's example, Northview developed and disseminated a literacy framework. Professional development was designed based upon the framework and classroom data. The district's literacy group came to understand that the *specific* strategies staff select are of secondary importance. The more important factor is consistency. For staff, the key ingredients for literacy success are that they *agree upon strategies that are research-based, effectively teach those strategies, and consistently use them with all students.*

Staff Conversations

A Conversation with a Middle School Principal, Andy Scogg:

Feel the Energy!

Teachers in Northview claim they have been "Fisherized" meaning that they have adopted Doug Fisher's recommendation to have a clear, concise, and powerful literacy plan. Northview staff believed that they could have similar results. Fisher's message helped them redefine the district's strategic plan around a cohesive literacy focus.

Northview's middle school principal, Andy Scogg, could not contain his excitement and pride in his staff's literacy work. "The district-wide focus on literacy is awesome—you can feel the energy in every building. It's gotten us on the same page; we are all so connected. It has moved our efforts greatly. We deliver consistency to kids. We don't offer twenty different examples of how to do something like note taking. It has brought teachers together. We offered demonstration lessons on vocabulary strategies and every seventh and eighth grade teacher voluntarily attended it during their planning time. We want to keep this literacy focus and just sharpen the saw. Nothing matters as much to our effort as getting teachers together to have conversations about instruction. We are just taking baby steps, but even though our number of socio-economically disadvantaged students nearly doubled over the previous six years, our achievement scores are going up. I think we are doing a better job of meeting kids' needs and teaching them than ever before.

The literacy framework solidifies the school system's beliefs. "A literacy framework implemented school wide can provide teachers with an opportunity to focus their teaching rather than script it, resulting in students who read, write, and think at impressive levels" (Fisher, Frey, 2007, p. 32).

The participation of staff in the development of Northview's literacy framework fostered ownership and sustainability. It is a research-based document that communicates expectations for quality literacy instruction in every classroom and every building. The cornerstone of the school system's literacy focus, the framework creates accountability for implementation. The literacy framework provides a solid grounding for instruction from which staff can take off and fly, and all students' achievement can soar to new heights.

• *What happens to us individually and collectively when we develop a common understanding of our professional practice?*

• *What are the benefits of establishing a literacy and/or instructional framework for student learning?*

• *What are the benefits of establishing a literacy and/or instructional framework to professional practice?*

Chapter 7

Implementation

Tough Question:

• What works?

Key Learning Principle:

• There are no silver bullets.

Main Ideas:

• Scientific evidence is fundamental to planning effective instruction.

• We blend best practices together with our own instructional expertise to address our unique populations of learners.

• It is the repeated practice of research-based strategies and our expertise that bring us long term improvement.

Best Practice

Scientific evidence needs to be a fundamental part of teaching. We must continually ask ourselves these questions:

- Will this instructional strategy work?

- Has it been proven scientifically to work in other places?

- Has it been proven not to work in other places?

- Can I expect it to work with my population of learners?

Those practices that are proven to lead to quality literacy teaching and learning are called "research-based practices." These scientific research-based practices have been studied and data collected to determine their effectiveness. Teachers who are serious about their professional craft use research-based practices as the foundation of their instruction. They weave these best practices together with their own instructional expertise in "what works" with their unique population of learners. The following two charts identify research-based best practices and common ground themes related to best practices in literacy.

Key Learning Principle

There are no silver bullets.

Effective Literacy Instructional Practices

Rasinski and Padak write about effective literacy practices that are applicable no matter the age of the student. They suggest the following:

"1. Share your own enthusiasm for reading and writing . . .

2. Read to students. Research has demonstrated that reading to students has a number of positive effects on reading: students who are read to have better comprehension and more extensive vocabularies than students not read to. In addition, reading to students is associated with successful early reading, with positive attitudes toward reading, and with greater awareness of what fluent reading is like . . .

3. Growth in reading is fostered best when literacy learners are engaged in real, authentic reading activities—read real books, magazines, articles, etc. for real purposes . . .   continued next page

4. Provide time for reading/Increase students' reading. It's really quite simple; people learn to read by reading . . .

5. Provide literacy rich environments for students. Research has found that environments for reading play an important role in students' growth in literacy . . .

6. Have high expectations for literacy learners . . .

7. Provide interesting language experiences for literacy learners. It is important that literacy learners develop a good background for the things about which they will read . . .

8. Connect reading and writing. . . . Reading provides writers with interesting ideas and models of good expression to use in their writing. Writing forces readers to get inside words and ideas in ways that require greater analysis and depth than when reading . . .

9. Tap into students' interests. Readers are more likely to read, and read successfully, those texts that are about things in which they have an interest . . .

10. Establish instructional routines. Routines are blocks of time during which certain predictable types of activities occur . . ."
    (Rasinski, Padak, 1995, p. 1-5)

Common Ground Themes Related to Best Practices (in Literacy)

Morrow, Gambrell, and Pressley identify common ground themes related to best literacy practices in their publication, *Best Practices in Literacy Instruction* (2003) as the following:

"1. Learning is meaning making.

2. Prior knowledge guides learning.

3. The Gradual Release of Responsibility Model and Scaffolded Instruction facilitate learning.

4. Social collaboration enhances learning.

5. Learners learn best when they are interested and involved.

6. The goal of best practice is to develop high-level, strategic readers and writers.

7. Best practices are grounded in the principle of balanced instruction."

Research-Based Best Practices (for Literacy) and Common Ground Themes Related to Best Practices (for Literacy) (Morrow, Gambrell, Pressley, 2003)

Persistent Implementation of our Whole Repertoire

Our pilot brings to the cockpit a set of scientifically based skills and practices that have proven results for safe, timely flying. His pilot preparation required the study of principles of physics as they relate to best practices for FLIGHT! He also learned the most effective techniques in manipulating the huge flying machine at his command. His profession demands strict adherence to these practices with each and every FLIGHT!

Our pilot uses these practices like clockwork. He reminds us of his colleague, James Sullenberger, who in 2009 landed the US Airways Flight 1549 in the Hudson River, with no fatalities. "Sully" has 40 years of flying experience; his style is cool and unflappable. To this he adds his intuition, general knowledge, and all the research he has done on airline safety.

Our pilot, like Sully, blends all those assets into an entire repertoire of professional practice. He uses the entirety of his repertoire to bring each and every FLIGHT! successfully to its destination. The accumulation of safe, timely completed FLIGHTS! builds both the reputation of the pilot and airline: this is an airline you come to trust to get you to your destination. Over time, with this track record, your confidence, and repeated business, the airline is considered an industry exemplar.

In education the use of best instructional practices is touted repeatedly as a requirement for improvement. The rationale for their use is easy to understand: we use what is proven to work. Given the strength of this argument, it is tempting to assume that best practices may be "the ticket" to improvement nirvana. The simplicity of this thinking is seductive. It leads us to the mentality of "the silver bullet" wherein we assure ourselves that this one tactic for improvement is the sure road to success. However, let's reconsider our pilot. He uses his *whole* repertoire of practices, not just those that are research based. He employs every appropriate tool, *depending upon conditions,* to produce a smooth as silk FLIGHT!

Sharratt and Fullan suggest in *The Schools That Did the Right Things Right* (2005) that as educators we can further our improvement efforts through our commitment to blend all of our practices together into a holistic approach. It is imperative to use both our scientific and experiential "know-how" with precision and persistence over time. It is the repeated practice of research-based strategies *and our expertise*, in alignment with our goals, that bring us improvement for the long term.

Northview's instructional efforts run parallel to what good companies do to achieve greatness, as revealed in Jim Collins' (2001) extensive research. He found that improvement is not wrought from one defining moment or activity. As hard as he looked for "the one big thing," Collins could not uncover a single event or moment that provided the leverage for improvement.

Jim Collins found that great companies had used practices and processes over time that could be described as:

- evolved
- gradual
- organic
- cumulative
- and developmental.

Collins states in *Good to Great* (2001, p.169), "There was no miracle moment. . . . Rather, it was a quiet, deliberate process of figuring out what needed to be done to create the best future results and then simply taking those steps, one after the other, turn by turn of the flywheel. After pushing on that flywheel in a consistent direction over an extended period of time, they'd inevitably hit a point of breakthrough."

The journey to success for all of the companies was characterized by the steady accumulation of effort over time. Additionally the leadership showed how the incremental steps of progress related to the overall goal (vision/mission) which engenders energy of staff, stimulating further momentum. Collins calls this the "Flywheel Effect." He continues, "People can just extrapolate from the momentum of the flywheel for themselves: 'Hey, if we just keep doing this, look at where we can go!'" (2001, p.177).

In Northview, best practices are very important. So is maintaining a district-wide focus on literacy, as well as ongoing, job-embedded adult learning. And don't forget the system. All of these elements are critical for turning, turning, turning the wheels of improvement. Everyone works on all of these practices intentionally over time.

In his book *Good to Great,* Collins (p.169) writes, "There was no launch event, no tag line, no programmatic feel whatsoever. Some executives said that they weren't even aware that a major transformation was underway until they were well into it," and, "The good-to-great companies had no name for their transformations." In Northview, we called it "Taking FLIGHT!"

Northview's administrators and staff were well down the runway of "Taking Flight!" in their collective commitment to the literacy focus. In *The 21 Indispens-*

able Qualities of a Leader, John C. Maxwell (1999, p. 51) titles one of his chapters "Focus . . . the Sharper It Is, the Sharper You Are." Administrators recognized their special opportunity to improve Northview's instructional focus as a vehicle to "sharpen" or improve the district as a whole—the students' achievement, the staff's instructional expertise, families' involvement, and the entire community's commitment to literacy.

Administrators and teachers had analyzed the data, surveyed staff, reviewed recommendations, and were convinced this was the most effective and powerful choice for the district. They now had to operationalize what it means to "implement a literacy focus."

As Richard DuFour states (2008), ". . . Even the most morally impeccable statements are ineffective as collective commitments if they do not establish clear expectations about what each person is expected to do to fulfill the commitments. . . . When educators articulate collective commitments, they should get down to the nitty-gritty details: What do we promise to do, today, to support our colleagues and our students?" (pp. 158-159).

To implement the literacy focus, the Literacy Leadership Group worked with administrators, staff, and district curriculum council. The implementation plan provided:

■ Clear, concise communication about the Northview literacy focus by:

- Distributing a letter from the Superintendent and Board of Education to all staff to rally support

- Sharing of the research on the importance of literacy to all content areas and student success in life

- Delivering a common message at all staff meetings by the Superintendent and Director of Instruction

- Providing presentations by Literacy Leadership Group as part of professional development days

- Sharing information with parents and the community via the district newsletter, The Northview News, the local press, and updates in building newsletters and on the district website.

- Displaying graphics, projects, and charts of literacy work in the buildings and in the Board of Education meeting room, to expose the public to literacy happenings of the district.

■ Supports for Students and Parents:

- Many schools bought multiple texts to support content reading.

- Teachers encouraged student selected texts based upon their interest and reading levels.

- Many schools instituted additional intervention and enrichment opportunities for students. Some designed them along the idea of the "book club" model to reinforce the social nature of learning.

- Late bus transportation was made available so students could obtain additional intervention or enrichment.

- More tutorial assistance and community mentoring was established, especially at the middle school, to provide more targeted service to students.

- Greater attention was drawn to the needs of special populations, especially special education students and economically disadvantaged students. More collaboration between general education and special education teachers was occurring with more sharing of strategies and resources. A greater emphasis was placed on parent involvement in literacy work.

- Classroom libraries were significantly expanded with a goal that each teacher had one, regardless of the content area they teach. Greater selections of fiction and non-fiction were added to accommodate student interests and reading levels.

- Communications went to parents sharing resources such as, "How to Read with Your Child," "How to Help Your Child with Vocabulary," etc. Presentations about the literacy focus were shared at monthly PTC (Parent-Teacher Committee) meetings.

- Some elementary principals offered workshops, donut and coffee meetings before school, and tips on how to build your child's literacy skills.

- Special literacy events were sponsored such as plays, book clubs. read-ins, Young Author's Celebrations, trips to the local library, literary events such as Shakespearean plays, poetry reading, etc.

- A community book club was sponsored wherein students, staff, and families read a common book, at multiple reading levels, and met to discuss.

■ Supports for Staff:

- A literacy coaching model was instituted. Initially three part-time literacy coaches were named to support their colleagues through demonstrating lessons, modeling, and providing professional development opportunities.

- Northview joined the Kent Intermediate School District (KISD) Literacy Coaching Network to join with other literacy leaders around the county. This dynamic group led county efforts and provided an excellent forum for sharing and growing in literacy expertise.

- Foundation funding provided additional collaborative opportunities and professional development funding for district literacy leaders.

- Volunteer literacy leaders were identified in each building. They worked closely with the literacy coaches.

- The Language Arts Committee and Literacy Leadership Group assembled a handbook for each teacher to clearly communicate the literacy framework, provide common vocabulary of terms, and provide resources to teachers in all content areas.

- Question and answer sessions were available to teachers to clarify and assist them in understanding the literacy focus.

- Literacy strategies were tailored to each teacher's content area.

- Literacy Coaches and principals assisted teachers during PLC, grade level, and department meeting time to help analyze and interpret data.

■ Time:

- Staff meeting time was often reconfigured by principals for literacy initiatives. In many buildings, literacy leaders helped design the learning. In other buildings, staff shared and rotated responsibility for presenting an effective literacy strategy to colleagues. Staff conveyed their needs and wants for use of the time to accomplish literacy goals.

- Release time: Teachers had the opportunity to utilize substitute teachers for working on implementing the literacy focus for their classroom. For example:

— Several middle school teachers met to plan "centers" where individualized and small group literacy activities could take place.

— Some Northview High School math teachers wanted to do "read-alouds" of literature and articles dealing with math concepts and design a method for all to use.

— Some elementary social studies teachers wanted to find literature selections that could support the literacy focus linked to social studies concepts.

— Some art and music teachers met with their colleagues from other grade levels to determine how they might support the literacy initiative. Out of this was born one high school art teacher's "Words of the Week" program whereby students graphically designed a key vocabulary word of the week for their fellow high school students. (See Features from Chapter 3).

— Conferences and Workshops: a priority was given to attending conferences that dealt with literacy issues

— District-wide professional development centered on the literacy focus.

— Many classrooms carved out a silent reading time daily. In some buildings it was first thing in the morning; in others at a consistent, designated time of the day.

■ Resources:

• The Superintendent, Northview Education Foundation, and The Ball Foundation supported purchase of professional books to support literacy instruction for teachers. Titles were suggested by teachers and were purchased for the teacher to keep.

• Professional libraries were expanded to include additional copies of requested literacy references.

• Each building received a dollar amount (approximately $1,000-$1500) per building for purchase of classroom library and/or teacher read-aloud selections.

- Local and national bookstores were asked for donations of books, magazines, and newspapers for student use.

- The community was invited either to donate or purchase books for the schools.

■ Leadership Considerations:

- Administrators discussed literacy leadership skills at their Ad Team meetings. They read articles, exchanged ideas, and came to common agreements. They identified resources needed to accomplish this role.

- "Literacy Learning" sessions helped administrators understand aspects of the literacy framework so they could lead efforts.

- Concrete examples of literacy initiatives in other districts were shared to provide models of best practices in literacy.

- The staff in each building was encouraged to take leadership for literacy within their grade level, team, or department.

- The Literacy Leadership Group along with the Language Arts Committee served as ongoing resources for the district.

- University professors from Michigan State University, Aquinas College, and Calvin College served as resources for the Ad Team and Literacy Leadership Group. They served as critical friends and provided support and assistance.

- KISD, the local intermediate school district, collaborated with the Northview staff for support and to provide leadership training for administrators in literacy. They accomplished this by sponsoring national experts such as Doug Fisher, Nancy Frey, Bob Marzano, and Carolee Hayes.

Jim Collins, author of *Good to Great* (2001) inferred that often the activities that good companies engage in aren't overly dramatic or life-shattering. As mentioned earlier, he noted that their practices scaffold over time to create greatness. So, too, it was in Northview. No one dramatic event occurred that transformed the district. It was everyone's consistent efforts, the attention to detail, the multiple levels of communication, the involvement of the stakeholders, and all the ways that it implemented the literacy focus that propelled the district on a trajectory to powerful instruction.

• *Where do we turn to find out "what works"?*

• *Why is scientific evidence critical in planning instruction?*

• *How might our own experience and intuition influence instruction?*

PART 3:
FLIGHT! to Adult Learning

To achieve high quality literacy instruction in all content areas, K-12, Northview developed a dynamic process for adult learning as expressed graphically below.

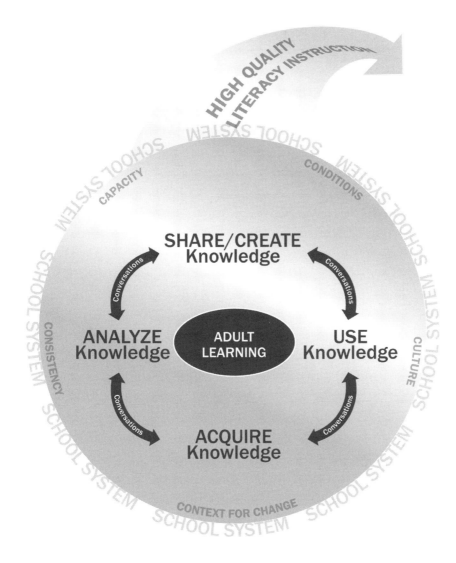

Chapter 8

Adult Learning: The Engine

Tough Questions:

- Why is adult learning as important as student learning?

- How do adults learn?

- What is a desirable balance for professional learning using experts, shared learning, and individual learning?

Key Learning Principles:

- Learning is social.

- Learning about the needs of our students enables us to match our instruction.

- The learning is in the difference (Rogers, 2003-2005).

- Most of the knowledge we need resides within the system (Rogers, 2003-2005).

Main Ideas:

- Adult learning is the engine that grows the individual and the school system, expanding their capacity.

continued next page

continued

- Information is the fuel for the engine, adult learning.
- The learning of adults impacts the quality of instruction.
- Four major factors influence adult learning:
  - Interest
  - Experience
  - Opportunities to learn
  - Motivation
- We learn incrementally by building on what we know and making subtle changes in our practice.
- We create new knowledge by questioning our beliefs and thinking in new ways.

*O*ur pilot is required to attend training on a regular basis to maintain and increase skills in the cockpit. As travelers our lives may well depend upon his commitment to this learning. As educators we, too, are responsible to sharpen our skills for the classroom. There is no disputing the high correlation between teacher effectiveness and student achievement.

Research indicates that expert teachers are the most important resources schools have to increase student achievement. Mike Schmoker (2006, p. 10) relates, "Instruction itself has the largest influence on achievement (a fact still dimly acknowledged)." As teachers we can track our students' learning, but we are left to guess how we may impact their lives when they leave us. According to Wilkins, citing details of the U.S. Government's education plan (Education Week, 2009), the suggestion is made that good teachers not only affect the learning and the learning environment of students, but more significantly the *life* environment for students. How do we build our capacity so that every one of our students can learn to their highest potential, and also "learn to fly" as an individual and productive citizen?

Adult Learning

Adult learning is the *engine* of the school system that simultaneously grows the individual staff member and the entire system, expanding their capacity and propelling them upward.

Information is the fuel for the engine. Conversation provides the spark to ignite the information, rendering it useable as fuel. As depicted in the graphic at the beginning of Part 3 (page 75), professional conversations are the vehicle for adults to acquire, analyze, share, create, and use information (or knowledge). This is an intentional learning process that influences the progress the entire school system can make.

The importance of adult learning, the learning of all the adults in the school system, places it directly at the center of the system as depicted in the graphic. In school systems that recognize the power of adult learning and establish a professional discipline to promote and structure it, adult learning can occur whenever professionals come together.

Examples of adult learning opportunities may include:

- two teachers simply discussing a lesson
- teachers participating in an educational blog about their instructional practice
- a mentor and new teacher sharing tips on classroom management
- a PLC (professional learning community) group reviewing assessment data
- principals and a superintendent conferring about instructional issues
- a teacher observing a colleague modeling an instructional technique

The adult learning graphic provides a model that underscores the social nature of learning; all components of the process involve staff learning *with and from* one another through their professional conversations.

This part of the book may well be the most important. It is about the learning of the adults in the school system. Adults are not simply learners in bigger bodies. Adults approach their learning somewhat differently than youth because of their accumulated experience. Honoring the special needs of adult learners has a profound impact on their ability to improve instruction and impact student achievement. *The learning of adults enables staff to improve instruction, which can then positively impact student learning.* It stands to reason, if adults are learning, so will students.

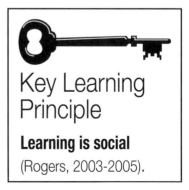

Key Learning Principle

Learning is social
(Rogers, 2003-2005).

The Northview Story Continues

In the late 1990's a minor catastrophe hit the district. Northview staff, K–6, had agreed to implement a standards based report card system. It was a computer based model for grades one through six that required teachers to input their grades according to standards.

An urgent call came in to then-Assistant Superintendent, Michael Stearns requesting his presence at an emergency meeting at Highlands Middle School regarding the implementation of the new computerized report card. The calamity resulted from a glitch in the software that had erased all the teachers' input, yet report cards were due to parents in just a couple days. The ensuing uproar rang loudly throughout the entire district. Teachers complained to the union, vowed not to re-enter the data, requested release time to get their report cards ready, and asked to return to hand written report cards.

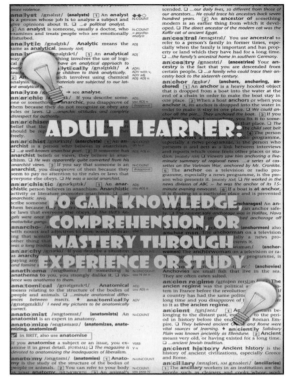

Student Art Work by Kassy O.

Fast forward to 2004 when Northview staff were surveyed and asked the following questions:

- Are you confident with using data?

- Has Northview taken the appropriate steps to help teachers use data and apply it to help students?

Most survey respondents indicated a positive response to these questions. How was it possible from 1998 to 2004 that Northview teachers became more pro-active about using technology and data? The answer lies in the district's recognition of the power of adult learning.

Staff Conversations

A Conversation with Kathie Lewis, Middle School Teacher and Adult Learner:

My Learning is Key to Improving Student Achievement

Kathie Lewis, a middle school teacher in Northview Public Schools, describes a teacher's continual learning as critical to improving student achievement. She says teachers normally strive to find ways to improve their instructional practice and recognize that they are never done. "I considered myself a good teacher at the outset of the initiative between Northview and its partner, the Ball Foundation. I varied instruction to meet the needs of diverse learners, developed creative and engaging lessons, and held high expectations for my students and myself. I also consulted with grade level peers about curriculum. However, I did not regularly meet with my colleagues to collaborate about best practice, review formative/summative data, or discuss student remediation, enrichment, or differentiation opportunities. Although I found great success with students, my focus was more about my teaching content than student learning."

"The work of the district and its partner, the foundation, stimulated a culture of learning," according to Kathie. "Teachers are district instructional experts and have been encouraged to have the confidence to improve our practice by holding sophisticated professional conversations to seek better ways to meet student needs. We have really pushed each others' thinking, and I'm really proud of the work we've done." Kathie says, "No instructional plan is ever finished. It needs to be continually revisited, refined, and improved based upon the results we are getting in student learning. We continue to realize not only our own potential as adult learners, but more importantly, the promise our learning holds for students."

Kathie Lewis attributes the growth of the professionals in her district to the processes of adult learning. Because teachers came together to engage in inquiry, dialogue, discussion, and reflection, teachers were catapulted forward in what they were able to accomplish. She comments, "The journey wasn't always easy or smooth. We could achieve better results learning together rather than working alone."

Over time, Northview recognized the importance of the following factors to adult learning:
- interest
- experience
- opportunities to learn
- motivation

INTEREST

Adults are interested in their learning when they perceive that it will increase their ability to deal with problems that they face in their work situations (Knowles, Holton III, Swanson, 2005). It stands to reason then, that teachers are interested in their own learning when they see the correlation to increasing the achievement of their students. An example of learning based on interest was Northview staff's

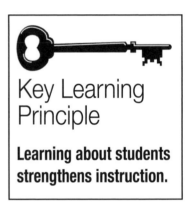

Key Learning Principle

Learning about students strengthens instruction.

response to the widening gap of student achievement within the classroom. Teachers expressed frustration in trying to meet the growing breadth of student needs, and they were eager to find solutions.

In response, the superintendent and district literacy leaders dialogued with staff about the range of student achievement. They also discussed the potential of data-driven literacy instruction to address these challenges. Soon the staff came to understand that data-driven literacy instruction was everyone's responsibility.

EXPERIENCE

Adults approach learning with different experiences, both in quantity and quality than young students. These experiences prove to be the most influential resources in adult learning (Lindeman, in Knowles, Holton III, Swanson, 2005). Therefore, to maximize the learning of adults, experiential techniques such as conversations, case methods, and actual problem solving activities tend to be the most effective strategies.

When we learn new information that is in sync with what we already know and believe, we call that "single loop learning" (Argyris & Schon, 1974) or incremental learning. Northview interpreted incremental learning as the learning of new skills and capabilities through gradual, step-by-step improvement. The result is doing something better without examining or challenging underlying beliefs and assumptions. Because this new learning closely aligns with existing knowledge, we are easily able to assimilate it and take it to action. Incremental learning requires us to ask questions within our existing framework of experience such as:

- What did we expect would happen?
- What actually happened?
- How will we change what we did for the next time? (Hinken, 2001).

Incremental learning is depicted in the following graphic:

Incrementally it grows the capacity of both the individual teachers involved and the school system. An example of an incremental learning experience might be high school teachers learning literacy strategies for teaching vocabulary in their content area. In this instance, teachers only had to change their practice slightly.

Incremental learning may lead to change in strategy but does not provoke a fundamental shift in beliefs, principles, or values. It can be described by activities that add to the knowledge and competency base of the school system without altering the fundamental nature of the school system's activities (Argyris and Schon, 1974).

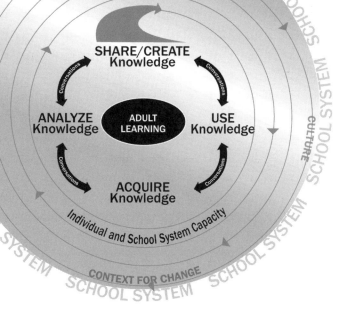

In 2000, Stearns and Grey realized that single loop learning or incremental learning alone was not able to take staff to the solutions they needed. It was also becoming increasingly apparent that the old habit of looking to district leadership for answers was no longer effective; they alone did not have them. Additionally it became obvious that problems were increasing in complexity and that simply tweaking current know-how provided only a partial Band-aid.

Stearns and Grey learned that they, along with other administrators, needed to assist staff in adjusting their expectations for quick fixes. According to Heifitz and Linsky (2002, p.15), "You have to counteract their (staff's) exaggerated dependency and promote their resourcefulness. This takes an extraordinary level of presence, time and artful communication, but it may also take more time and trust than you have." It was time to recognize the power of innovative learning (also called double loop learning). Innovative learning requires questions that:

- stretch the learner beyond their prior experience,
- result in the learners reworking their beliefs, principles, or values in a significant way,
- allow the creation of new ways of working,
- and promote the implementation of new strategies.

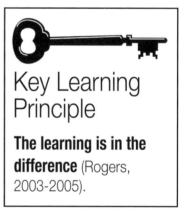

Key Learning Principle

The learning is in the difference (Rogers, 2003-2005).

Burson (from Hinken, 2001) suggests that creating innovative solutions requires that a school system ask questions such as:

- What are we doing that causes this pattern of poor performance to continue to happen?

- What makes us think that our action strategies will actually result in the improvement we seek?

- What beliefs do we hold that cause us to value this intended outcome in the first place?

Innovative solutions cause us to reshape the underlying patterns of our thinking and behavior so that we are capable of doing different things. This level of learning may spring from incremental learning but takes the learners to a new, higher level of functioning. The learning required in innovative solutions is depicted in the graphic that follows.

According to Knowles et al. (2005, p. 190), "The most effective practitioners are those who are good at double-loop learning." It is this learning for innovative solutions that grows the knowledge set of the learner and stretches the capacity of the school system. It is also referred to as "breakthrough learning" (Fullan, 2005) or "adaptive learning" (Senge, 1990) and (Heifitz, 2002) and can take an entire school system very quickly into a higher state of effectiveness.

The creation of innovative solutions takes our thinking to places we have never gone before. *It stretches our boundaries and expands our capabilities. When we share our knowledge with one another, we are exposed to thinking that differs from our own.* Lurking in the gap between the thinking of others and our own thinking is unlimited opportunity for creation of new ideas and growth. We discovered that "the learning is in the difference." This understanding became yet another key principle which enabled us to value divergent ideas. We gradually came to see our differences and varied perspectives as *desirable resources* rather than potential obstacles.

As Northview staff analyzed student achievement data, they experienced some unsettling realizations about literacy and the need for change. This information challenged their beliefs about student learning and caused them to think in new and different ways about instruction. The district intentionally provided structured opportunities for processing in their PLC's. These constant conversations gave rise to new knowledge and understandings which generated a new excitement for sharing and learning. It ignited enthusiasm and promoted the district's effectiveness to improve student achievement.

**Staff
Conversations**

**A Conversation with Anita Flynn,
First Grade Teacher:**

*"We Talk with One Another, Make Connections, and
Create New Solutions. It's Almost All We Need."*

"When Superintendent Mike Stearns first brought a
group of Northview staff members together to plan for
a meeting with our foundation partners, it was the
first time this particular team had met. Our task was
to agree upon what practices were proving particularly
effective across our grade levels. It took us quite a bit of
conversation to agree upon common ideas. Mike wanted
us to focus on our use of data, specifically our data
warehouse. After we shared ideas, we began to view our
promising practices (K-12) in different ways and understand they were linked together.

As we talked about our use of data, we really struggled.
It still didn't mean much to me. I had never understood
my part in it. But as we talked about what the data
warehouse was for, what it could do for teaching practices, I began to create a picture of how all the parts
fit together. By the end of the meeting, we had begun
to make new connections, clarified our ideas, and understood how each of our parts made up the whole. We
really came together as a team.

Through our continued conversation we discovered that
the data warehouse wasn't useful for many teachers,
especially elementary school teachers. Many of us had
never been involved in defining what we really need or
in designing a warehouse.

We suggested creating our own data warehouse for elementary schools. At the follow-up meetings, teachers,
and staff came up with new thinking to make the warehouse useful. There was a need for text and images,
not just numbers. We were working with the technology
people on how to make this happen. We know it will

> help focus our instruction and strengthen the process of becoming a stronger learning community. The opportunity I was given to participate on this district team changed how I have been involved in district initiatives. Our conversations with one another were a powerful impetus to discover our common ground, discover creative new solutions to our issues and needs, and realize our ability to meet them collectively."

Although confusion arose from innovations, patterns of improvement surfaced.

For example, the first iteration of the data warehouse was a disaster and of little benefit to teachers at all. Yet it sparked conversations about how to use data. Additionally, a standards-based grading system for grades K-6 floundered several times, but staff persisted in developing a creative teacher-friendly solution through their professional conversations with one another and their administrators. Also, many staff regarded the time spent developing a district-wide theory of change as a colossal waste. However, the theory of change eventually became an accepted guidepost for all change initiatives.

OPPORTUNITIES TO LEARN

"A school district that is not continually learning is a dying district," Mike Weiler, a former superintendent, used to passionately remind his staff. "Learning is not only the end goal for students; it is our means to the end for the entire school system." We consider student achievement as the primary measure of our success. If our students have learned well, they pass muster for higher education and productive citizenship. If our students have learned well, we assume we have taught well.

There is a high positive correlation between student learning and our instructional practice (Marzano, Pickering, Pollock, 2001). *Therefore, it behooves us to become students of our own practice, since the better we teach, the more our students can learn.* In order to improve our practice we must continually be learning about it. This is an important construct because it expands our thinking about the role of teaching.

With the advent of the federal government's "Response to Intervention" or "RTI," educators scrutinize their instruction to ensure that it will best match students' needs. RTI comes from the reauthorization of the Individuals with Disabilities Act (IDEA), the legislation that defines federal rules for special education. Response to Intervention has reshaped the educational landscape with its intent to decrease the number of students who are classified as students with disabilities. The law calls for a variety of assurances; perhaps foremost is the early identification and intervention with students who are struggling readers. Intensive evidenced-based early intervention is also prescribed and each student's progress is monitored via data-based documentation.

Richard Allington suggests in his book (*What Really Matters in Response to Intervention*, 2009, p.115) that he would like to see the name of RTI changed to, "Response to Instruction." He states, "Good teaching is adaptive teaching. It is adapting the standard lesson in ways that make it fit the reader (or readers) in front of you. Adaptive teaching, then, requires that teachers are paying close attention to what their pupils do and say as they move through a reading lesson. No two lessons are really ever exactly alike because students differ, and even groups of students differ, from each other." He continues,

> One of the key features of the best teachers we studied was the size of their instructional toolbox. When a lesson, or a set of lessons, wasn't producing the targeted learning, these teachers would figuratively reach back into their toolbox and pull out a different way to teach decoding or summarizing or self-monitoring. The less effective teachers we studied seemed unable to do that.

Critical to building all teachers' toolboxes of effective instructional strategies is attending to the learning of *these* adults, the teachers. Mirroring Allington, we draw our focus to instruction. No longer can the role of the teacher be thought of as simply "teaching." Instead, an inquiry of a teacher, "What *do* you do?" should evoke the response, *"I teach (my students), and I learn (about my instructional practice)."* Alverado and Fink (in Wagner, Kegan, Lahey, Lemons, Garnier, Helsing, Howell, Thurber Rasmussen, 2006, p. 114) state, "If it's not about teaching and learning, it's not about anything."

When the system develops intentional ways for adults to learn, both structured and spontaneous, it creates the engine, or power source for the organization. It is a more complex way of thinking about "training" or "professional development." In the traditional approach to providing learning opportunities for teachers, we have attempted to "educate" them. This term emphasizes the "educator," the agent of change who presents a body of knowledge for learning and designs activities for learning.

The locus of control is outside the teacher since most often the school district has determined "what teachers need to know." Gradually we must recognize that teachers themselves can determine what they need to know about their own practice, especially if they have access to quality, timely information, or *data*, about their students' performance. Indeed, given the time and structure, teachers can govern their own learning, aligning it day to day with the unique needs of their students.

In Northview, the implementation of the data warehouse provided just-in-time-information that allowed teachers to determine students' needs. Staff could then develop an aligned instructional plan for not only their students, but also their own learning needs.

MOTIVATION

Does everyone want to be in charge of their own learning all of the time? What we know about adult learning is that motivation to control one's own learning is situational. Many of Northview's adult learning efforts shifted from formal, directive professional development events to collaborative learning in PLC's. For the most part staff responded very positively to their newfound autonomy. In collaborative groups teachers were charged to:

- determine what they needed to learn,

- accomplish that learning goal through sharing practices with one another,

- adjust and coordinate instructional practice based upon their new learning,

- and assess the efficacy of that learning by analyzing student results.

The autonomy involved in self-determined adult learning certainly sparked a great deal of staff energy. They viewed it as evidence of the administration's confidence in their instructional ability and trust in their positive relationships with one another.

However, self-directed learning did not satisfy all staff which is predictable given the variability of individual approaches to learning. We were reminded

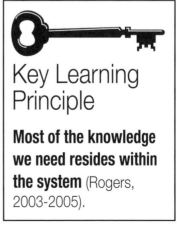

Key Learning Principle

Most of the knowledge we need resides within the system (Rogers, 2003-2005).

of the old metaphor for learning: the campfire, the watering hole, and the cave. In this comparison, traditional professional development is compared to gathering around the campfire to soak up the knowledge of a revered expert. The watering hole represents teachers gathering together, as in PLC's, to learn with one another. Finally, the cave represents the classroom to which teachers retreat to answer their own questions and pursue their individual learning—alone. Knowles et al. (2005) call out four types of learning which we related to this metaphor in the table below.

Four Types of Learning

Venue	Type of Learning	Locus of Control
Anywhere	Unintended learning	No control
Campfire	Authority-directed learning	Authority controlled
Watering Hole	Shared, self-directed learning	Shared control among learners
Cave	Individual, self-directed learning	Learner controlled

The research of Brookfield (1983) suggests that there is a need for balance between the authority-controlled and learner-controlled learning. In a shared control model for learning, it is desirable for the learners to create their own learning in order to establish motivation and a sense of community, as well as to validate the desirability of the activity and materials.

Shared control can take many forms, limited only by the imagination of the participants. Examples include professional learning communities, communities of practice, peer instruction, team learning, and collaborative evaluation. Fullan and Sharratt, in *The School District That Did the Right Things Right* (2005), suggest that a requirement of an improvement effort is that new strategies should be learned in context. These collaborative formats for self-directed learning provide such job-embedded learning.

Shared, self-directed learning allows a school system to tap the expertise that resides within. Internal experts cost less, are easily accessible, and are known quantities, making them desirable resources for professional learning. However, we need to also respect the need for outside perspectives as in "authority-directed learning." We may require the objectivity of those who are not entrenched in our own system. Herein is one of the values of a critical friend who can pinpoint the chinks in our armor invisible to us.

We must admit that there are sets of knowledge that we do *not* have and need. It is no admission of inadequacy to seek outside resources for learning. In fact, although we honor the knowledge that resides within a system, we purport that a school system's capacity is expanded with the provocation of external authorities or experts. They bring in a set of concepts outside our existing understandings. We invite them to the campfire where they challenge us to stretch and grow. Once again we are reminded that "the learning is in the difference."

Finally, we value the process of learning that takes place in the cave. Day to day in the classroom, our students present us with new information which we reflect upon individually, connecting it to what we already know. Those connections often enable the development of new understandings and applications, never previously considered.

Many of us have spent the bulk of our professional lives in our respective "caves." We have been sprung from that setting with the recent realization that most learning is a social process. Learning with peers and sharing accountability for growth is both stimulating and liberating. Currently, shared learning, or the watering hole, is enjoying tremendous attention as *the* professional development venue of choice. We are wise to keep the pendulum in check recognizing the value of all three formats. A balance between the campfire, watering hole, and cave should be enlisted for acquiring the knowledge needed to meet students' needs.

Staff Conversations

A Conversation with Kathie Lewis, Middle School Teacher:

We Teach and *We Learn*

Kathie Lewis shared, "Our partnership with the foundation began to challenge teachers' commonly held view of professional development as an individual activity. In this view teachers chose their own training and applied the learning according to their individual levels of motivation, without any district standard of accountability."

Kathie continued, "Our foundation partners began to inquire about the possibility of planning teachers' learning as a direct correlate to student achievement strengths and gaps. They helped us wonder about the possibility of intentionally linking teacher's learning to the district's

(continued)

school improvement effort wherein teachers not only set goals for student achievement but also set goals for their own learning and assess *their own* results in terms of students."

This required a major shift in thinking about professional development. If tied to student achievement, professional development could no longer be an event. It needed to be an ongoing process wherein teachers continually learned about their professional practice in the context of students' needs. Framed in this way, the learning of the adults was elevated to new heights; it became as important as our students' learning and redefined our role as teachers.

"We were now not only teachers, we were learners, too." Kathie continued, "It was initially foreign to us to see ourselves as teachers *and* learners. Any district that takes on the challenge of change will encounter bumps in the road and must persevere. Initially, some of us resented not going out of the district to work with experts on topics of interest. We still are all at different places in our understanding of our expanded role of teaching and learning, but we are much further down the road toward greater student achievement than when we began. The (PLC) process provides the structure and the opportunity to come together around our instructional practice. Adult learning processes give us the tools to make that PLC time productive."

Adult Learning at the Watering Hole

Northview's PLC teams had been evolving across grade levels, departments, and administrative teams. It had become apparent that professional conversations would not take place regularly without a structure. The logistics of getting people together took lots of creativity. We had to rethink how we use our time and other building resources including contract language. Once PLC's were established, our partner, the foundation, watched teams in action and listened to staff conversations. As our thought partner, they pushed us to consider how we, as adults, learn. They made us question: "We are coming together in PLC's, but are we learning?"

According to Senge (1990, p. 236), "If teams learn, they become a microcosm for learning throughout the organization. Insights gained are put into action. Skills developed can propagate to other individuals and to other teams. The team's accomplishments can set the tone and establish a standard for learning together for the larger organization."

Over time the foundation's emphasis on the potential of learning with and from our peers led us to the realization that most of the knowledge we need to move forward resides right within our own district. We recognized that when we share our knowledge with one another, there is little we are unable to accomplish. We just needed ways to unlock our own potential.

When Commander Sullenberg landed Flight 1549 in the Hudson River, he received innumerable kudos for his skillful execution of the landing. He was lauded for his quick thinking. Surely he demonstrated a cool calm demeanor in extreme danger. "Sully" was the epitome of courage as he walked the aisle, not once, but twice to make sure all passengers had deplaned. Everyone escaped this life threatening calamity with few injuries incurred. Commander Sullenberg deserves every bit of acclaim he has received. However, he did not work solo to affect a positive ending to this aborted FLIGHT! He worked with his crew to bring the passengers to safety. Although we heard little about the efforts of the FLIGHT! attendants, they, too, were instrumental in guiding passengers to safety. Strapped in their own seats, they loudly coached passengers to prepare them for a water landing.

The entire crew *worked as a team* to ensure the safety of their passengers. Together with Sullenberg, they accomplished what is considered an aviation near-miracle. No power, no control tower, no landing strip. Yet within their own ranks, they had what they needed to get the job done.

• •

• *How do we foster learning that matters for the adults in the system?*

• *Why is adult learning so important?*

• *What is the difference between incremental and innovative learning? How can we stimulate both kinds of learning?*

• •

Chapter 9

The Learning Cycle

Tough Question:

- How can we best learn together?

Key Learning Principle:

- Connect the system to itself (Rogers, 2003-2005).

Main Ideas:

- When teams learn collaboratively, it is helpful to consistently employ a model of the learning process.

- "The Learning Cycle" suggests that collaborative learning is a dynamic process.

- "The Learning Cycle" is comprised of five components:

  —Use knowledge

  —Acquire knowledge

  —Analyze knowledge

  —Share/Create knowledge

  —Employ professional conversations

*P*ilots are always intentional about safely arriving at their destination. So too, in schools, teachers must be intentional, heading in the "right" direction, aiming for increased levels of student learning. Responses to Intervention (RTI), No Child Left Behind, PLC's, and just the use of data, have caused teachers to think about the importance of their own learning as well as the learning of their students. Many teachers are finding themselves in not just a "knowing, doing" gap but a "help me know, then help me do" gap. Teachers are seeking to improve their instruction. They want support to *know what to do* and *how to do it*.

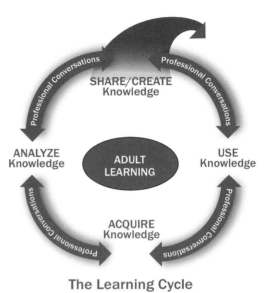

The Learning Cycle

Increasingly teachers are taking responsibility for their own learning. They are reorganizing their time to learn and the way they learn. They are finding value in introspection on their own instructional practice and they are tapping their colleagues' knowledge.

Educators are asking probing questions such as some suggested by Rick Wormeli, in his book *Fair Isn't Always Equal: Assessing and Grading in the Differentiated Classroom* (2006, p. 183):

- How does assessment inform our practice?

- How can we counter the negative impact of poverty on our students' learning?

- How can we provide feedback to students most effectively and efficiently?

- Do our assessments provide us with the information for which we are searching? If not, why not, and how can we change them so that they do?

- How are our current structures limiting us?

- Whose voice is not heard in our deliberations?

- What do we know about differentiated practices and the latest in assessment thinking and how are those aspects manifest in our classrooms? If they are not, why not?

- Are we doing things just to perpetuate what has always been done?

- Are we open to others' points of view—why or why not?

- How does my grading approach get in the way or support students' learning?

- What will our grading and assessment practices look like fifteen years from now?

Wormeli refers to the above questions as "big questions." He says, "Responding to the big questions re-centers us, helps us identify where to spend our energy and resources, and also helps us make stronger commitments to one another and our school's programs" (p. 182).

In Northview as teachers increasingly used their data and asked questions, we noticed a pattern in the way we were learning in our authentic literacy work. We paired this pattern with principles of adult learning and created a model called, "The Learning Cycle," only to discover that others had come before us.

Our model of adult learning looks very similar to the models of Kolb (1984) and a variety of others. However, our emphasis on the social context of learning makes our model unique and particularly strong with its tight alignment to research on adult learning (Knowles, Holton, Swanson, 1998). Our model emphasizes the pervasive, social component of adult learning—professional conversation, which we discuss in Chapter 10.

We call our model "The Learning Cycle" because the term "cycle" suggests that collaborative learning is a dynamic process. As in most educational processes we can start where it makes sense and follow it everywhere.

The Composition of the Learning Cycle

The Learning Cycle is comprised of five components:

- use knowledge
- acquire knowledge
- analyze knowledge
- share/create knowledge
- employ professional conversations

Let's assume that you are a high school teacher and are wondering how this model might bolster *your* learning. You are scheduled to meet with your learning team (PLC or whatever you may call it) at the end of the week, and you want to prepare for productive use of this time. Consider thinking about the model in this way:

COMPONENT 1: USE KNOWLEDGE

Your team has been teaching a literacy standard on vocabulary. This represents *using knowledge*, since you are using your instructional expertise to teach the big PLC curriculum question, "*What* do students need to know?" This part of the cycle assumes the knowledge of instruction, too: "And *how* will I teach them?"

COMPONENT 2: ACQUIRE KNOWLEDGE

After instruction, it is imperative to determine how students responded to your instruction. The team administers a common assessment to gather information about students' learning. This is the component of the cycle in which you *acquire knowledge* of student results. It can be in the form of an authentic performance, or local, state, or nationally normed assessment. Your team may also identify additional data or assessments that may be needed.

COMPONENT 3: ANALYZE KNOWLEDGE

Equipped with student data, you are ready to move to the cycle's third component, *analyze knowledge* in which you answer the PLC question, "How do we know students learned it?" It is here that your team engages a series of tools including inquiry, dialogue, listening, and reflection with which you analyze student learning in a sophisticated manner. The conversation that ensues will answer the questions:

- What does the data show?

- Who learned?

- Who did not?

- What patterns do we observe?

This conversation generates understanding about student successes and student needs.

COMPONENT 4: SHARE / CREATE KNOWLEDGE

Share knowledge is the part of the cycle where the team shares what they know about instruction from their experience, as well as observation and intuition (Gladwell, 2005). This sharing makes the team's collective knowledge about effective practice accessible to all. In this part of the learning cycle, your team decides what strategies might work best for your population of students. Questions stimulate the conversations:

- What worked?

- How do we know?

- What did you do to help your students be successful?

- What did not work?

- What would we do differently next time?

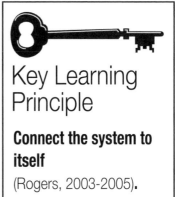

Key Learning Principle

Connect the system to itself

(Rogers, 2003-2005).

Create knowledge is the component of the Learning Cycle that takes us to new, higher levels of functioning. This is where the creation of innovative solutions takes place. According to Gregerman (2007, p. 23), "This (creating new knowledge) occurs when we test the bounds of other peoples' best thinking against the needs of our customers (students). . . and wander beyond the boundaries of what we already know."

It is important to realize that most new knowledge is built upon something that already exists, using something that someone else has already done as a springboard. Our job is to find or create instructional strategies that work and implement them in ways that truly matter to our students. Achieving innovative solutions requires an understanding of what our students need and what is important to them. This necessitates willingness to suspend judgment and ask tough questions about what we know and what could be.

These questions might sound like:

- What can we do to be more successful with students?

- What might reach our students?

- What have others tried with students similar to ours?

- What novel ideas might just *work*?

- What do we need to create?

Staff Conversations

A Conversation with Diane Kuhn, Special Education Teacher:

Peers used my suggestions. Better yet, they worked!

As Diane Kuhn, a special education teacher at West Oakview stated, "In our PLC group a question arose about how to best help a particular student in a third grade regular education classroom. Because I had experience with the challenge and had tried strategies that proved successful, I shared them with the third grade teachers. A week later when we met, the teachers related that they had tried my ideas, and they worked. Without these opportunities for conversation, we wouldn't be working so closely together and sharing ideas, needs, and strategies with each other. We all benefit because of the spirit of sharing. And so do our kids."

Northview had begun to learn that when we share our knowledge with one another across grades, buildings, and roles, we are connecting the system to itself with information about *what works, what does not, and how we can create more powerful instruction.*

Component 5 of the Learning Cycle, Employ Professional Conversations, is so vital to adult learning that the entire next chapter is devoted to it.

"Take-Aways"

• *What is the value of thinking about professional learning as a discipline such as in the "learning cycle"?*

• *How can we intentionally "connect the system to itself"?*

• *Under what circumstances do we learn most powerfully about our practice? What are the implications for our system?*

Chapter 10

Professional Conversations

Tough Question:

- What happens if we work to understand rather than be right?
  (Wheatley, 1992).

Key Learning Principles:

- Listening is often more important than speaking.
- We are better together than we are alone (Covey, 1992).

Main Ideas:

- Teachers' roles have changed from individual workers to membership in a community of learners.
- Professional conversations shift the emphasis of professional development from growing the individual to the whole team.
- Professional conversations foster teachers taking ownership of their own learning, individually and collectively.
- Five tools of professional conversation include:
    - Setting norms   - Inquiry   - Reflection
    - Listening   - Dialogue

COMPONENT 5 OF THE LEARNING CYCLE: PROFESSIONAL CONVERSATIONS

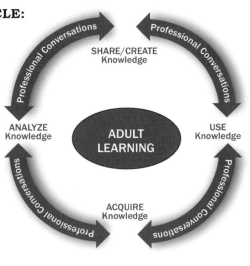

Doug Fisher, nationally recognized literacy expert, relates, "We believe that it takes time and collegial conversations to develop a shared vocabulary of teaching and learning and these conversations spring from a habit of reflective teaching. In other words, it is not a program, a set of books, or a box of materials that creates a high achieving school. It is always teachers who matter, and what they *do*, matters most" (Fisher and Frey, 2004, p. 3).

There has never been a more critical time to foster teacher collaboration and shared learning. How often do we hear that teachers are isolated? They are so busy and have so many demands that they walk into their classrooms, shut the door, and practice their craft—alone.

In many ways, No Child Left Behind (NCLB) has had a major influence on freeing teachers from isolation. To meet the rigorous demands of the legislation, teachers have rallied, circled the wagons, and put their collective heads together.

Where do schools find the time and how do they provide support for collaborative efforts? Many teachers in Northview attended the Professional Learning Communities training sessions in the Midwest or received training from their building colleagues. Those trained heard Rebecca DuFour describe how her school creatively captured time for professional learning communities to meet. She and her staff "banked time" by saving extra minutes of the week to create big blocks of time that teachers could use to work collaboratively. She also shared that all adults reviewed their schedules to make sure they fostered student learning, rather than adult convenience.

Northview teachers were inspired to be creative in finding common time to meet with colleagues. Elementary teachers approached administrators with new ideas. They recommended innovative ways to use all the adults in the building and suggested organizing their specials (art, music, foreign language, and physical education) into blocks of time to create common planning time for same-grade level teachers to collaborate as a PLC group.

On one occasion, elementary students attended a play in the high school performing arts center. The principal, guidance counselors, and teachers of all the specials were responsible for students in the auditorium, while common grade level teachers held social studies content meetings in the spacious coat room of the auditorium. Teachers teamed with other colleagues and shared students for special events. Their "buddies" time occasionally afforded common time for grade level teachers to collaborate. Principals also stepped up to the plate, offering to take a teacher's class so they could work with colleagues.

Northview's middle schools and high schools already had time built into their professional schedule for collaborative time. Teachers had planning periods designated as time to work with their grade level, content area, or department colleagues. Principals gave teams additional time if needed to collaborate with teachers in another building often by using rotating substitute teachers that could be shared by multiple teachers.

There was a culture developing around collaboration. Teachers made use of tools of quality instructional practice and organized themselves into collaborative learning teams. They were also trained in listening, dialogue, inquiry and reflection. These tools allowed teachers to collaborate in a synergistic way that shifted their role from an individual working alone to a well-developed community of learners.

One of the best ways for teachers to learn and improve their instructional practice is through professional conversations. Professional conversations are what it sounds like when everyone is a learner to an agreed upon end, in this case, instructional practice. Professional conversations are the vehicle for social learning. They shift the traditional orientation of professional development from helping the individual to growing the capacity of the team and school so that the needs of all students can be better met.

Student Art Work by Talita P.

Professional conversations unleash the potential to solve increasingly complex problems as teachers discover new skills, insights, creative ideas, or points of view. Ideally these conversations transpire pervasively throughout the district. They are appropriate for every setting and structure, from dyads to large teams. They represent an *intentional*, respectful way of working to improve instruction and increase the learning of both adults and students. Professional conversations are considered an *essential* facet of adult learning.

Professional conversations honor teachers' ability to be responsible for their own learning and to share what they know. When Northview designs opportunities for teachers to come together around instructional issues, the district validates the very fact that teachers have something to offer—that indeed, the answer lies within the teacher and collectively the staff.

Northview soon discovered that bringing adult learners together around student learning does not necessarily result in improved practice. In the beginning stages of the work, they assumed that the PLC structure was sufficient to promote teachers' learning. Staff found that they needed additional tools and training to have meaningful conversations around student achievement. Our Ball Foundation partner, Brayman, observed, "Great effort has been devoted to getting people into groups and giving them time to meet. However, training is rarely provided in how to converse meaningfully. Conversation is the core process of learning together."

Staff Conversations

A Conversation with Mark Thomas, High School Principal:

We Need a Shared Approach to Collaborative Conversations

Mark Thomas shared that a Northview staff member had commented to him, "We have systematic ignorance on conversation, and we need a shared common approach." Mark continued, "Teachers are asking for a framework for structuring collaborative conversations. In the early stages of the PLC work in Northview, people were put into groups but the district fell short of helping them to know *how to have conversations* and on a simple level *what to have conversations about.*"

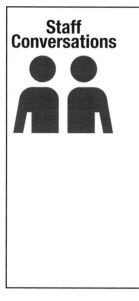

Staff Conversations

A Conversation with Andy Scogg, Middle School Principal:

Making Progress

According to Andy Scogg, principal of Crossroads Middle School, "Until we began to make the time to hold professional conversations, we were stuck in frantic activity. When we took the time to talk about what matters, listened to one another, and asked hard questions, we began to make rapid progress. So long as we are taking the time to talk in a systematic way about increasing student achievement through improved practice, we will continue to make gains. In fact, *conversation may be our most important work.*"

Tools for Professional Conversations

Northview teachers came to understand that their conversations need to be grounded in trust (norms) and in specific tactics that invite all voices to be heard and understood (listening). They needed the license to tackle hard questions without drawing immediate conclusions (dialogue). They needed powerful questions to drive hard conversations about what works and what does not (inquiry). And they needed time to think about what their conversations mean to their practice, collectively and individually (reflection).

What follows is a set of tools for adult learning that fosters effective, efficient professional conversation used with the adult learners in Northview. The reader will recognize these tools; they are commonly referenced and most of us have at least some understanding of them. However, just knowing about something does not guarantee quality application. We provide a brief overview of these tools for professional conversation and suggest the reader practices them collaboratively to achieve the greatest results.

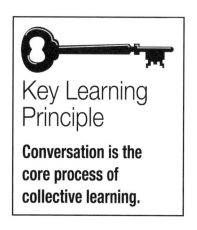

Key Learning Principle

Conversation is the core process of collective learning.

PROFESSIONAL CONVERSATION TOOL 1: SETTING NORMS

Definition: Norms are standards that guide how the group interacts and works together.

In the early days of Northview's collaborative PLC work, unanticipated problems cropped up. The reality was that some teachers dreaded going to team meetings. At times, colleagues came in late. It was possible for one person to dominate the conversation. Unable to voice their opinion, other teachers left feeling frustrated. Some appeared to just "check out," waiting silently until the meeting ended. Often the conversation bounced between individuals' agendas. Various staff would leave wondering, "What was that all about?" wishing they had stayed in their own classroom to get "something important" done.

Northview soon discovered that every formally established group needs norms for interacting. Norms, sometimes called ground rules or operating principles, facilitate the teams' collaborative work. They are critical for getting things done. Typically they address communication issues, help build rapport/relationships, and provide group-work guidelines. They provide a standard for behavior that gives predictability to the teams' interaction. Predictability, the capacity to predict another's behavior (Bennis and Nanus, 1985), is the foundation for trust. Predictability is generated when the group creates its own operational principles and holds itself accountable for them. People tend to trust one another when they know where they stand in relation to one another and to the organization.

Northview teachers found it advisable to establish norms at the outset of each team's development so that predictability is established as "the order of the day." Most teams need considerable history with one another before they develop a sense of community. A set of norms can unite the team in respect for one another until such time as the team establishes a collaborative identity.

As in any relationship, the way team members interact with each other changes as more time is spent working together and learning about each other. Many areas improve, but new issues emerge constantly. It is a natural part of team development. Effective teams take the time to address issues as they surface, to "tune-up" the ground-rules they establish for interacting. This is an ongoing process.

Many teachers agreed that norms should be posted publicly for the group's easy reference. The following are examples of procedural norms that Northview teams developed or used:

Example 1—Our team commits to:

1. Starting and ending on time.

2. Sharing talk time equitably.

3. Using data as well as our experience in decision making.

4. Holding one conversation at a time.

5. Respecting the opinions of all.

6. Using consensus decision making.

7. Rotating design of the agenda.

Example 2—Our team commits to:

1. Being respectful of one another and maintaining confidentiality.

2. Being willing to consider matters from another's perspective.

3. Listening attentively.

4. Maintaining a positive outlook and attitude.

5. Committing to active participation in learning.

6. Setting aside judgment; being open-minded.

7. Keeping cell phones and other electronic devices silent.

Example 3—The following are additional examples of some norms that teams utilized (Garmston, Wellman, 2002, p. 47):

1. Putting ideas on the table: Ideas are the heart of a meaningful dialogue. Labeling the intention of our comments promotes understanding. For example we might say, "Here is one idea" or "One thought I have is. . . ."

2. Paying attention to self and others: Meaningful conversation is facilitated when each group member is conscious of self and others and is aware of not only what she/he is saying, but also how it is said and how others are responding.

3. Presuming positive intentions: Assuming that others' intentions are positive promotes open communication and eliminates defensive or judgmental mindsets.

PROFESSIONAL CONVERSATION TOOL 2: LISTENING

Definition: Listening is a process of attending to make meaning.

Listening is a process of attending: taking in the speaker's words, non-verbal behaviors, and what is *not* said in order to make meaning of the entire message. It requires the physical process of hearing in addition to the intentional effort of comprehending what is said. True listening is a statement of caring. When we listen, we work so hard to understand another that we suspend our own mindset to accommodate theirs.

Student Art Work by Brooklyn V.

A point made by Margaret Wheatley in her book, *Turning to One Another*, bears noting. "We weren't trained to admit we don't know. Most of us were taught to sound certain and confident, to state our opinion as if it were true. We haven't been rewarded for being confused. Or for asking more questions rather than giving quick answers. We've also spent many years listening to others mainly to determine whether we agree with them or not. We don't have time or interest to sit and listen to those who think differently than we do" (2002, p. 34). In many schools, too often this plays out. Time to listen, hear varied perspectives, and develop common solutions is often neglected.

Northview discovered there is no greater benefit that impacts student achievement than to have the adults in the school working collaboratively on instructional practice. According to Cindi O'Connor, one elementary principal, "Taking the time to intentionally develop listening skills pays off to this end." Wheatley (2002, p. 36) states, "We have the opportunity many times a day, everyday, to be the one who listens to others, curious rather than certain. But the greatest benefit of all is that listening moves us closer. When we listen with less judgment, we always develop better relationships with each other. It's not differences that divide us.

Key Learning Principle

Listening is often more powerful than speaking.

It's our judgments about each other that do. Curiosity and good listening bring us back together."

Teachers were given the time to meet for purposes of collaboration. When principals and teachers intentionally worked on listening skills, it enhanced the value of the PLC processes. Prior to this focus on listening skills, many Northview teachers admitted that often there was a lack of understanding about the focus of the meeting, who should be contributing, or what the intended outcome of the meeting should be.

Teachers and principals structured the improved use of listening skills as parts of every meeting. They did not need to go out of their way to create special opportunities. Grade level meetings, staff meetings, department meetings, and school improvement meetings provided authentic forums for applying listening skills.

Teachers especially found the format for paraphrasing from the Center for Cognitive Coaching extremely helpful (Costa, Garmston, Ellison, Hayes, 2005, p. 37). In the first type of paraphrase, the listener initially acknowledges and clarifies what the speaker is saying. Once the speaker "signs off" that that is what he/she is saying, the conversation continues. In the second type of paraphrase, the listener sums up and organizes what the speaker said. The listener may say something like, "You have two plans here that you are considering; one is _____ and the other is _____."

The third paraphrase links the focus of the speaker to something he highly values or believes in. It may sound like this: "So, you really believe strongly in . . ." or "It's obvious you highly value . . ." For Northview staff, paraphrasing at all levels proved to be an excellent strategy to improve the quality of the listening skills.

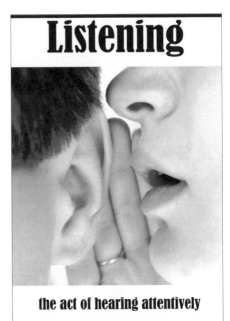

Teachers at all levels found that simply paraphrasing the speaker's ideas back to the speaker improved their:

- listening skills
- appreciation of each others' perspectives
- recognizing others' rationale for their opinions.

Student Art Work by Rachel L.

Staff Conversations

A Conversation with Sheridan Steelman, High School English Teacher:

Listening Is a Starting Place for Improvement

Sheridan Steelman, a Northview High School course leader for English 9, contributes, "We are working on teams sharing everything, really listening to each other's perspectives and ideas, coming to agreements, and pitching in. The quality of what we are doing collectively for students is so much better. Many teachers feel we are having our best year ever." Intentionally developing listening skills proved to be a starting place for much of the district's improvement.

PROFESSIONAL CONVERSATION TOOL 3: DIALOGUE

Definition: Dialogue is a process of suspending judgment in order to understand others.

Peg Luidens and Marilyn Tabor (1999), learning consultants, developed a chart, which we adapted, that depicts "What Makes a Difference in Adult Learning?" Luidens' work was generated from the research of Bruce Joyce and Beverly Showers (Joyce and Showers, 1995, p.112) and clearly speaks to the power of coaching adults and/or engaging in professional dialogues:

What Makes a Difference in Adult Learning?

Activity	Knowledge and Understanding	Ability to Use New Skill	Application in Daily Practice
Theory	90%	25%	5%
Demonstration	90%	50%	5%
Practice/Feedback	90%	90 - 95%	5%
Coaching and/or Professional Dialogues	95% – 100%	95% – 100%	90%
Reprinted with permission of author.			

When staff are coached and/or engage in professional dialogue, their ability to know and understand a concept and skill is consistently high. It is also high in situations where theory alone is presented, a demonstration is conducted, or a practice with feedback session is provided. The *significant difference* among adult learning activities is in what teachers actually *apply* in daily situations.

The percentage of application to daily practice jumps from 5% to 90% with the addition of coaching or opportunities to dialogue. With these interactions, teachers have the opportunity to exchange ideas. They clarify their thinking, make meaningful connections, and come to a deeper understanding of new knowledge. They make the learning their own. When teachers collaborate with other teachers, it dramatically increases the likelihood that there will be *application* in *daily instructional practice.*

Staff Conversations

A Conversation with Tricia Hampel, Elementary Principal:

Dialogue is At the Heart of Adult Learning

Tricia Hampel, elementary principal, reports, "Using effective dialogue techniques helps teachers and administrators figure out what can effectively work to help a student. As a result, honest and open conversations occur. Many related issues around curriculum alignment, instruction, and assessment come up in the dialogue sessions. Teachers report that it has made a difference in impacting student achievement and that they, indeed, share and apply what they learn." She is delighted when she hears teachers say, "Hey, I tried that idea, and it really worked, not just with the one student, but with all the students in my class." She firmly believes dialogue and conversation are at the heart of adult learning. "I see both working every day. They made a huge difference for our staff and students."

She continues, "New teachers would remark that they had never thought of that idea and were grateful for the suggestions. Staff end up learning and sharing new

(continued)

> strategies, and we consider *all* kids *our* kids. We collec-
> tively approach solutions when a student's performance
> puzzles us. We feel a great sense of collegiality. There is a
> feedback loop built into the program so we can follow up
> on suggested strategies to see what worked. We have our
> support staff members sitting in on the meetings, and
> they are welcome to share observations and suggestions.
> It has really made the PLC processes more meaningful.
> Now teachers have a method that helps them have deep,
> focused conversations."

Glenna Gerard and Linda Ellinor in the publication, *Dialogue at Work: Skills for Leveraging Collective Understanding* (2001, p. 1), state, "Conversation is the magic in organizations. . . .The practice of dialogue lies at the heart and soul of organizational learning, the term 'dialogue' comes from the Greek phrase *dia logos*, which means 'through meaning.' That is, dialogue is based on the idea of people coming together to create collective understanding."

Gerard and Ellinor explain the difference between discussion and dialogue and characterize dialogue in an interesting way (p. 2). "When learners participate in dialogue, observers would notice that speakers and listeners are:

- expressing a desire to hear what all present have to say,

- listening deeply especially when they disagree with one another,

- seeking to identify each other's assumptions about issues by asking clarifying questions such as, 'Could you tell me more about how you arrived at that conclusion?',

- speaking at a slower pace, often punctuated by pauses, as they reflect on what they're hearing,

- and trying to understand how all the different perspectives fit into the big picture."

In contrast Gerard and Ellinor explain that "*discussion*" is people tending to come with their thoughts and agenda items, often without giving attention to others' needs, issues, or a larger goal. In most discussions, individual opinions often take center stage and many times listeners readily evaluate the comment by thinking something like one of the following:

- "It might work."

- "It won't work."

- "We've tried that before; hang around and that idea will go away."

Northview had experienced the shortcomings of strictly holding discussions. Often decisions are made hastily for the sake of efficiency. In discussions, one person can easily monopolize the time, leaving some group members without the opportunity to share their ideas or thoughts. Another danger of discussions is that people can leave frustrated, with a feeling of being left out and with a sense that their voice is not valued and not heard. A further weakness of discussions is that there is no protocol for handling conflicts or disagreements when they arise, so decisions may be made by the loudest, strongest, or most powerful member of the group. Clearly in discussions, it is easy to comply just to bring the issue to closure.

Key Learning Principle

We are better together than we are alone
(Covey, 2003).

One Northview teacher states, "We *want* to go beyond surface discussions. But we are caught up in the 'tyranny of the urgent,' i.e., we want a product right now and don't want to be slowed by conversations laced with conflict. But just because there is a different perspective or different opinion, doesn't mean it has to be fraught with conflict. We need to learn to focus on the *work*. *None of us have been trained to have those conversations.*"

PROFESSIONAL CONVERSATION TOOL 4: INQUIRY

> ***Definition: "Inquiry is an approach to learning that is active, focuses on questioning, critical thinking, and information seeking" (Hubbard and Power, 1998).***

Inquiry typically involves both individual and collaborative reflection on and analysis of learning. Inquiry can lead teachers to a new understanding of themselves as teachers and of their students as learners.

Our Ball Foundation representative, Brayman, reminded us that "our questions are often more important than our answers." Through the process of inquiry we can ask questions that provoke analysis of learning and stimulate our imaginations.

Inquiry is not so intent on producing the "right" answer because there seldom is just one. Instead inquiry serves to discover the availability of assets and the resolutions to complex issues.

Inquiry needs a discipline that recognizes:

- the context of the conversation (What do we need to know?)

- a framework for questions (What are the key concepts we need to explore?)

- different levels of questions; questions that begin with "what" usually evoke a technical answer; questions that begin with "how" usually stimulate more adaptive responses.

Participants need to develop their own questions to align with what they need to know. The following are examples of inquiry questions Northview developed with its foundation partner to analyze student achievement and professional learning needs:

Knowledge Acquisition

- What do we need to know? How can we focus on the assets of the situation?

- What kinds of information/data will assess that? What are we currently using?

- What role can parents and students play in supplying needed information?

- Is our data timely enough to impact instruction?

Knowledge Analysis

- How did our students do on the assessments?

- To what do we attribute their level of performance?

- Does the level of performance indicate the need for change in curriculum or instructional practice?

Knowledge Sharing/Creating

- What information needs to be shared and who needs it? Is this a grade level, building, or district issue?

- What do I know that works?

- Who else has an effective strategy?

- Who else might need to know this?

- How can this information best be shared?

Knowledge Creating

- What else might we try that is out of the realm of our current strategies?

- What makes us think that our action strategies will actually result in the improvement we seek?

- Why do we value the intended outcome in the first place?

- What could we do to turn any pattern of poor performance around?

Knowledge Use

- What have we learned?

- How might it affect my practice for the short term/long term?

- What are our agreements going forward?

- What follow-up conversations do we need to have?

The following questions are examples of inquiry about professional development:

- Given our student performance goals what might we need to learn about our instructional practice?

- Are our professional learning activities aligned with what we have learned from data?

- Do we respect the fact that most of the needed "wisdom is in the room"?

- What are the limits of our collective knowledge?

- Who might be able to stimulate our thinking and expand our collective knowledge?

- How do we find a balance between learning from individual experience, our peers, and outside experts?

- What structures will foster learning from one another and outside experts?

PROFESSIONAL CONVERSATION TOOL 5: REFLECTION

Definition: Reflection engages the teacher in the process of thinking, pondering, and noticing. It often causes a pause in talking. This gives way to revising ideas, questioning, clarifying, reinforcing, and visualizing.

John Dewey, educational reformer, reminded us that we do not learn from our experiences; we learn from *thinking* about our experiences. Reflection is an essential tool that causes teachers to think about what their conversations mean.

Mark Twain viewed the act of reflection in this way: "Reflection is the beginning of reform." Reflection is an integral part of adult learning. It is vital that professionals constantly and critically review their professional practice. Reflection can be a bit risky since it often causes one to challenge assumptions and stretch thinking, opening up new possibilities.

Northview recognized that reflection was critical to learning. In the words of one middle school teacher, "Through reflection we came to be more open not just to colleagues, but to students and parents. We realized our culture was changing; we were taking more time to analyze what it was that we were doing, match it to our results, and take opportunities to ponder better ways of teaching. We stopped to take stock of the results we were getting and used the information to work with our colleagues on better ways to teach and better ways to help students learn."

In *Reflective Practice to Improve Schools* (York-Barr, Sommers, Ghere, Montie, 2001), a Four-Step Reflection Process is suggested. Many Northview teachers found that these reflecting questions dovetailed with the stages of the learning cycle. Questions prompted their thinking about instructional practice and student learning.

1. What actually occurred? What did we notice? (knowledge acquisition)

2. Why do I think this occurred? (knowledge analysis)

3. What does this mean? How can I improve? (knowledge sharing and creating)

4. Now what? Next time, what do I want to do? (knowledge use)

The key to productive reflection is honoring the time we need to process information. So often we feel compelled to move to action. We want something concrete to show for our investment of time and energy. We need to be able to put another check mark on our to-do list. But teachers need time to think; they need headspace to figure out how the new information connects with what they already know and to make meaning of it for future use.

Staff Conversations

A Conversation with Middle School Teacher, Todd Visser:

The Power of a Disciplined Approach to Learning and Conversation

Todd Visser, who teaches middle school math, shares his insights about results achieved through team collaboration and use of adult learning processes, such as the learning cycle. Todd says, "We had all embraced the idea of using common assessments and having meaningful dialogue about them to improve student learning, but we had not exercised our courage to have those conversations. I encouraged my teammates to do so stating that I thought we really ought to take the risk of holding possibly uncomfortable conversations because the potential payoffs were so great. I explained that the actual processing of data should be relatively easy as we could use a simple spreadsheet, something already loaded on every teacher's computer.

Our math teachers came together and pushed through the fear of seeing their individual class scores compared to others. After conquering our anxiety, we were able to institute a consistent process. Today we do an item analysis on all unit tests. We contrast our test scores and results with those of our colleagues. We have meaningful conversation about student learning, about *all* students, in *all* classes. We pose questions to each other. We dialogue about our observations and push on each other about strategies we used to get the results we got. We reflect on our strategies and our results. We are always seeking ways to do a better job. I'm proud of our learning and our teamwork."

Todd and his teammates understand that there is no reason to change unless they get better results. They cite the processes of the learning cycle as key to their success. Without a rigorous process for team learning, without the conversations, without the courage to face whatever comes up in the conversations, change would not be possible. His team exemplifies the power of a disciplined approach to learning and conversation to push and clarify thinking, and come to a shared understanding of best practice. Through professional conversation, Todd and his colleagues:

- acquired their data

- analyzed their data

- shared their knowledge and created new, innovative solutions

- and planned and implemented their instruction based on this new knowledge to better meet student needs.

As Northview found throughout their transformative journey, adult learning connects the system to itself. Adult learning provides the power to improve instructional practice and releases the energy that lifts all participants to an even higher altitude on their FLIGHT!

• •

• How does it change the nature of relationships when we seek to understand rather than be right?

• What is the power of professional conversations?

• How can we intentionally grow our skill level with professional conversations?

• •

PART 4:
FLIGHT! to Systems Thinking

Northview employed five components of the system as agents of change. They are represented graphically below: culture, conditions, capacity, consistency, and context for change.

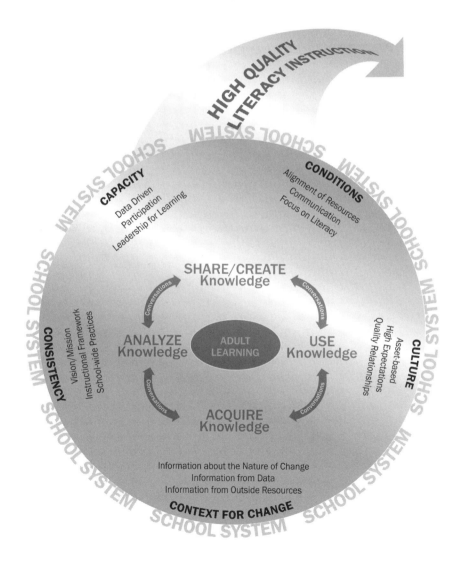

Chapter 11

What is a System?

*D*efinition: *The term "system" coins a way of thinking about an organization as a whole. A system pays attention to interrelationships and patterns of change. It attempts to determine how major functions influence each other and the behavior of its people. Systems work integrates available resources for change (Senge, 1990).*

"Systems offer us the possibility of becoming something different and greater than anything we had been" (Wheatley, Rogers, 1996, p. 41).

System Components:

- Context for Change
- Culture (Wagner, Kegan, Lahey, Lemons, Garnier, Helsing, Howell, Thurber Rasmussen, 2006)
- Conditions (Wagner et al., 2006)
- Capacity
- Consistency

In these days of diminishing resources and ever-increasing expectations, how do we use what we have to get the schools we need? One way is to think about our schools, not as a district nor as an organization—but as a school system.

The term "district" conjures up a definition based on geography and politics which narrows our thinking to issues of territory and governance—both only minimally correlated to quality instruction and high student achievement.

The word "organization" suggests sequence, hierarchy, and structure that exert control over processes and people. Problematic is that control can hamper the ability to respond to unexpected new demands in innovative ways.

A school that operates as a totally integrated "system" can increase the learning for both staff and students. When we think of our workplace as a "school system" we are able to create "dynamic connectedness" (Wheatley, 1990, p. 23) which fosters relationships and collaborative learning. This focus recognizes that all facets of the system are linked and that a change in one may very well impact others.

This type of dynamic connectedness links:

- the various components of the school system,

- adult learning,

- and the instructional focus, in this case, literacy,

- both within and beyond the school system.

The following chart explains the differences between districts, organizations, and systems.

Differentiating District, Organization, and System Characteristics

	District	Organization	System
Definition	• A territorial division for administrative or electoral purposes • Often based on geography and/ or politics	• An administrative and functional structure • The term is descriptive of personnel and/or structure of the group	• A regularly interacting or interdependent group forming an organic whole • A group linked by dynamic connections • Exemplifies a coherent body of ideas and principles (http://www.yourdictionary.com/system)
Sphere of Influence	• Usually impact is limited to those within the organization and its stakeholders	• Impact may be limited by conformity to the standards and boundaries of the organization	• Multi-dimensional and can include everyone at every level • Because of the interdependence associated with a system, the impact can extend in many ways both within and outside the system (Wheatley, 1992)
Roles/tasks	• Issues of territory and governance • Traditional leader(s) in control	• Hierarchical assignment of jobs, tasks • Control exists over people and processes • "Top-down" management and leadership • Roles are highly defined	• Those in the system view themselves as learners in collaboration with others in the system (Senge, 1990) • Collaboration is a key mode of working along with networking and shared leadership • Roles are loosely defined to promote flexibility

continued next page

	District	Organization	System
Methods of functioning	• Designated authority figures, a governing board or group • With power to set policy	• Predictable • Systematically planned • Directive methods of operation • Emphasis on efficiency	• Networks of people are active participants in creating a preferred future (Senge, 1990) • Are interdependent in their service to the vision and mission • Exhibit flexibility to respond to demands and change (Wheatley, 1992)
Potential to achieve results and attain vision and mission	• Actions are often contingent on the effectiveness of the existing leadership to affect change and sustain progress.	• Actions may be limited to "what we've always done" • May be limited by the leader's effectiveness • The ability to respond to unexpected new demands may be diminished (http://www/ehow.com/facts).	• Greater opportunities exist to achieve vision. • The system can adapt to meet changing expectations • Often may be more able to exercise high level change (Senge, 1990)

How can we think about the complexity of an entire school system as an orderly, manageable whole? Northview learned that the extent to which we purposefully aligned the system with the literacy focus determined the degree to which improvement of literacy instruction was developed, spread, and sustained.

Wagner, Kegan, Lahey, Lemons, Garnier, Helsing, Howell, Thurber Rasmussen (2006, p. 220) suggest that "every system is brilliantly designed to produce exactly the results that it does." The obvious correlate is that if we want to improve results, we need to change the system, too. But where do we start and what will make a difference?

By paying attention to the whole context in which they worked, Northview's administration learned a lot about systems. They recognized that change, as difficult as it is for some to assimilate, is simply a given. Yet instead of being a force to resist, they could choose to look upon change as a catalyst for learning and innovation throughout the system. Because of the need to respond quickly and nimbly to change, they were forced to loosen their grip on routine, outdated practices, and isolation. "We need the courage to let go of the old world, to relinquish most of what we have cherished, to abandon our interpretations of what does and doesn't work" (Wheatley, 1992, p. 5). Instead the leadership team learned to replace certainty with ambiguity, control with order, and hierarchy with inclusivity. More than ever they found that they needed each other's knowledge and wisdom to keep up with the constant demands from inside and out to adapt, create and relate. Responding to change, and trying at times to get ahead of it, was like competing in athletics with someone who is just a little better. It gave administrators a heightened self-awareness and an edge to their professional practice.

As the leadership team recognized the increasing number and complexity of demands on the school system they tried to figure out how to make sense of it all. They wanted to get off the treadmill of ever increasing pressure and rediscover serenity and confidence in our work. Was there a simpler way? What could happen if the system recognized its long held commitment to relationships? What might be possible if they began to foster connections between all members of the staff, not only for the sake of sociability, but also to grow the system to new levels of competence? And perhaps relationships between people were not the only connection. Maybe there was a relationship to be encouraged between staff and their own learning, between staff and existing resources, and between staff and information. "It is time to stop now. It is time to take the world off our shoulders, to lay it gently down and look to it for an easier way" (Wheatley, 1992, p. 17).

The administrators wanted above all to promote student learning to ever higher levels. They knew they were a "good" district, but greatness eluded them. They began to consider how to tap the relationship potential in the district. Wheatley (1992) admonishes leaders to view permanent structures within a system as silos that impose control and separate us from one another.

What the team discovered they needed was a system of processes that would facilitate flow of information and connect staff to one another and to key resources. In so doing they could evoke responses to questions of what happened and what might have worked better. By facilitating relationships they could create a context of pooling knowledge, skill, intuition, and resources to provide just in time quality instruction for each and every student. Wheatley writes, "Power in organizations is the capacity generated by relationships. It is a real energy that can only come into existence through relationships. . . . What gives power its charge, positive or negative, is the quality of relationships" (p. 38-39).

When the leadership nurtures interactivity in their system, they concurrently expect broad participation which builds individual and system-wide capacity. Staff's participation brings multiple data sets into play which enriches the quality of the decisions they can make. Simultaneously it generates the development of a collective reality to which participants are willing to commit. According to

Wheatley, "It is impossible to expect any plan or idea to be real to employees if they do not have the opportunity to personally interact with it. Reality emerges from our process of observation, from decisions we the observers make about what we will see" (1992, p. 67).

When leadership invites everyone to the table they are creating an open system, wherein staff can engage with one another inside the system and with colleagues in other systems (Fullan, Hill, Crévola, 2006). The flow of information remains fresh. Everyone is alerted to what is working, and what might hurt us, and then can respond accordingly. They learned that next to relationships, information is "king." It is only when a system does not have access to disruptive information that it is at risk. When a system does not have information about its own weaknesses, or is unaware of external challenges,

Key Learning Principle

When we align the system to our goals, we can attain them.

its stakeholders make uninformed decisions that can spell disaster. Wheatley suggests, "Open systems maintain a state of non-equilibrium, keeping the system off balance, so that it can change and grow. They participate in an active exchange with their world, using what is there for their own renewal" (1992, p. 78).

The leadership team also learned about the importance of creating shared meaning throughout the system. How can this be possible when everyone's participation brings such variability to the work? When everyone is encouraged to share what they know, what provides a sense of coherence? Throughout the system they discovered that the vision/mission, when developed by all stakeholders and communicated clearly and frequently (Bennis and Nanus, 1985), bound them all in a common quest. The vision/mission established a solid foundation for our day-to-day work and future goals. Throughout the system staff understood their raison d'être as individuals and as a collective. Through thick and thin the vision/mission became the basis upon which decisions were made. It was a consistent source of purpose, motivation, and fulfillment that everyone shared.

Over time it became clear that the system itself was a dynamic force that held great potential for learning as well as building the capacity of its stakeholders. However, the system remained a complex and nebulous entity. Wheatley's eloquent descriptions of a system, though poetic, held insufficient clues for application. How could we understand and talk about our system so that we could intentionally grow it and use it as a resource?

The Harvard Change Model (Wagner, Kegan, Lahey, Lemons, Garnier, Helsing, Howell, Thurber Rasmussen, 2006) helps a school system define key system components. We adapted their original ideas to represent our understanding of the Northview system components and their potential for improving achievement.

We had learned important theories about systems from Wheatley (1992) and Senge (1990). Yet it wasn't until we studied the system work from the Harvard Change Model, (Wagner et al., 2006), that we were able to use system thinking in our authentic work. Their model of a system depicts components which we could identify in our own system. In their model, they pinpoint four "C's" of a system: context, competency, conditions and culture. As we worked with these components we learned that we had to blend these with our own understanding; we could not simply transfer their model to our unique situation.

Senge et al., in *The Fifth Discipline Fieldbook* (1994), admonish that organizations cannot be transformed by simply transplanting someone else's model. It is fruitless to follow a prescription that belonged to someone else. It will only work when we interact with a model and create our own unique design.

Although the Harvard Change Leadership Model made great sense, it did not totally resonate with our recent learning. The development of our own systems model is an example of how we all see and understand the world differently. If they are to have utility, our innovations need to reflect our own reality. We can duplicate; we can generalize; but the most meaningful creations are molded from what we know from our own work.

We created a model of a system that mirrors two components from the Harvard Change Leadership model. However, it also includes three other components based on our research, knowledge and experience.

From our collective experience, we viewed the school system as comprised of five components (Wagner, Kegan, Lahey, Lemons, Garnier, Helsing, Howell, Thurber Rasmussen, 2006) defined below:

- **Context for Change** refers to the dynamic of living in a global society:

  - Knowledge is growing at exponential rates.

  - Information is instantly available.

  - Workplace demand for ever-increasing levels of education is rising.

  - Many children find themselves without the connection to and supervision of adults for greater parts of their day.

• Demographics are dramatically changing with increasing diversity and numbers of children in poverty.

School systems must be able to adapt quickly to demands in the way they teach and serve students. In fact, change may be the only constant we can count on.

■ **Culture** is the shared values and beliefs that guide behaviors and determine "the way things are done around here" (Sergiovanni, 1984). Culture is a prime determinant in how both students and teachers learn, how teachers teach, and in how leadership and the quality of relationships are defined.

■ **Conditions** include the focus a school system deems its most important work. It also takes into account ongoing communication as well as the tangible arrangements of time, space, and resources that influence student learning.

■ **Capacity** is the potential to learn and grow the skills and knowledge that influence learning. In this story capacity is grown in the areas of data-driven decision making, participation, and leadership.

■ **Consistency** is the predictability of behavior which builds trust (Vaill, 1989). When the vision and mission guide all decision making (Bennis and Nanus, 1985), everyone can trust that they share the same purpose and are heading in the same direction. Additionally, use of consistent instructional practices across the K-12 system correlates positively with student achievement.

As depicted at the beginning of Part 4, in Northview each system component targeted three strategies. All subsequent chapters in Part 4 will bring each system component and its strategies to life.

• •

• *What are the advantages of viewing our district as a system?*

• *How can we intentionally mine the system to attain the vision and mission?*

• *What system components hold the most potential for propelling the system forward?*

• •

Chapter 12

Context for Change

Tough Questions:

- Where can we get powerful information to fuel our learning?
- How can knowledge of change expedite implementation of initiatives?
- Why do we need critical friends?

Carry-On

Key Learning Principles:

- Things get messy before patterns emerge (Wheatley, 1992).
- Leadership is not role specific (Senge, 1990).
- Often we need to go slow to go fast (Rogers, 2003-2005).
- Sometimes we have to try something before it makes sense (Fullan, 2006).

Main Ideas:

- Understanding the complexities of the change process fortifies us to make necessary changes.
- Information from data and outside sources strengthens our decision making.
- The vision and mission provide stability and order in the change process.

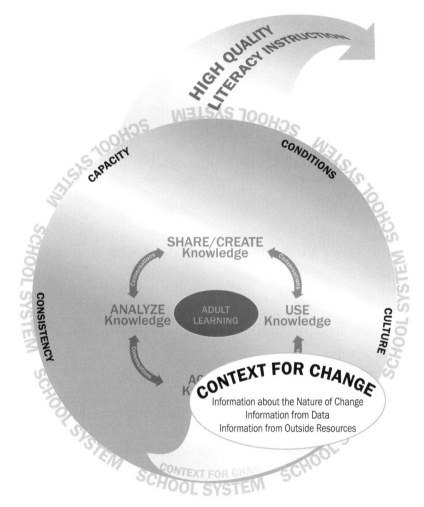

*D*efinition: *Context for Change refers to the dynamic of living in a global society*:

- Knowledge is growing at exponential rates.

- Information is instantly available.

- Workplace demand for ever higher levels of education is rising.

- Many children find themselves without the connection to and supervision of adults for greater parts of their day.

- Demographics are dramatically changing with increasing diversity and numbers of children in poverty.

School systems must be able to adapt quickly to all of these demands in the way they teach and serve students. In fact, change may be the only constant we can count on.

Just as pilots have to continually monitor the change in weather conditions to maintain the safest and speediest FLIGHT! path, so, too, do school systems need to continually monitor the winds of change in pursuit of their vision. Often those winds are turbulent, limiting a direct path. Given the wind's many directions, it is easy for things to get "messy" and to get lost along the way.

Margaret Wheatley writes, "Life uses messes to get to well ordered solutions" (Wheatley, 1992, p. 13). But, educators at all levels are planners who seek order and predictability:

- teachers do lesson plans,

- principals do school improvement plans,

- superintendents do strategic plans,

all with the goal of changing the school system to agreed upon ends. How, then, as consummate planners do educators reconcile their need for order with the requirements of system change?

The answer lies in the school system's knowledge of the relationship of information to its health and viability. A central concept for this book is that information is the fuel for the engine called "adult learning." It is our ongoing learning and increased understandings that are the catalyst for meaningful change. In order for a district to have ample information, we need to actively seek it from a multitude of sources.

Context for Change Strategies

- Information about the Nature of Change

- Information from Data

- Information from Outside Sources (Fullan, Hill, Crévola, 2006, p. 97).

Information about the Nature of Change

"I don't mind change as long as I don't have to do anything different." This unspoken feeling often pervades a school system. This was true for the staff of Northview as well. Even when change is based on a pressing need, a solid rationale and quality data, coping with change can be difficult. It helps considerably when staff explicitly understands the dynamics of change.

We studied the change process knowing that whatever changes were made would ripple throughout the system. The Northview administrative team developed a "theory of change" as a starting point for the implementation of the data warehouse. A "theory of change" is a set of principles that serves as a guide post for the implementation of a new process or program.

Northview learned that there are many sensitivities attendant with change, both at the system and individual levels. It became apparent that a few key understandings help facilitate the change process:

Theory of Change	Northview Response
Change should be based on shared vision, and it should be communicated with clarity to all stakeholders.	Northview engaged staff in the development of a mission statement so that everyone could understand and identify with it.
Change is experienced as a loss by many.	Northview honored the history and the culture of the district as it recognized that teachers truly wanted to do the best for their students. It gave teachers the time they needed to understand the advantages of using data to improve instructional practice.
There is often wisdom in resistance.	Administrators sought critical feedback about the data management system and continually listened to seek mutual understanding.
Changes should permeate the organization.	Changes were made system-wide with input solicited from every staff member.
Change is both individual and organizational.	While individual staff members began to use student data to improve their instruction, it gradually became a system-wide practice.
Evaluation is necessary to determine if the changes are resulting in positive differences.	Acquiring and analyzing data became critical to understanding the effectiveness of instruction.

(Houston, 2004, p. 1)

Northview worked hard to understand the dynamics of change. Change became a regular topic of discussion. What did making change mean at the macro level? How did change affect teachers' day-to-day work in the classroom? Northview found that changes seldom enjoyed instant widespread adoption but developed traction over time. Often we need to try something out before it makes sense. We need to take proposed changes from their conceptual state to implementation before we can recognize their value. We also are responsible to provide the resources, including time and training, required for successful application of the change. When we understand the nature of change and provide necessary support, change becomes an easier pill to swallow for the reticent and a source of inspiration for those who readily embrace the "new."

Information from Data

Wheatley suggests that when people participate with one another, sharing their information, creativity abounds and results in innovation. "Knowledge is generated anew from connections that weren't there before" (Wheatley, 1992, p. 115). "Through constant exchanges, new information is spawned, and the organization grows in effectiveness" (p. 116).

Stearns, Grey, and district administrators fanned out across Northview to gather data to improve student achievement. They asked:

- What are we doing?

- What results are we getting?

- What are the challenges students are facing?

- What barriers does staff face in developing the best in every child?

- What support would help?

- What are your major curriculum concerns?

- What takes a lot of needless time?

The goal was to get teachers talking about their daily practice in a non-threatening way. We purposely did not ask what changes needed to be made. We just listened. What came out of these discussions were three main concerns:

- the effect of changing demographics
- the widening achievement gap
- the lack of current information on students

As these conversations deepened, a realization dawned on all of us. Perhaps one solution could solve in whole or part all three issues. District leaders said to staff, "If we could find a way to give you current information about your students—would that improve your instructional delivery? Yes! Staff started discussing how this could happen—and the district began to coalesce around a way to manage data.

We observed that the more opportunities staff had for exchanging what they knew with one another, the more information they generated. When the staff felt their contributions were respected and valued at all levels of the system, they were motivated to share even more. The more knowledge they shared with one another, the more they were able to create new solutions and improve instructional practice.

Key Learning Principle

Things get messy before patterns emerge.

As a result of all this knowledge sharing, information overload often occurred for staff. It felt messy. How did staff bring coherence to all this new information?

We can handle the disruption of new ideas or strategies so long as we keep fixed on our ultimate goal. This is where the vision and mission of the system keep us on our common path. Our vision gives us a strong frame of reference for organizing our new information in a meaningful way. Integration of new information can take us to higher levels of effectiveness.

The more information that was available, the more it flowed from one level to the next. With increased openness in Northview, traditional hierarchies began to flatten. Titles became less important because everyone's voice was now important and had influence. No longer did staff see themselves as employees responding to top down decisions. Instead, they acted like equal partners taking up the banner of their collective mission.

Our conversations about data gave us information that allowed us to stay true to our vision and plan instructional strategies tailored for our students. We found that sharing our information with one another gave us the ability to flex what we did quickly and nimbly. Information built our capacity to keep our eyes on our students' future while planning "needs-based instruction" on a day-to-day basis.

"In this new world, you and I make it up as we go along, not because we lack expertise or planning skills, but because that is the nature of reality. Reality changes shape and meaning because of our activity. And it is constantly new. We are required to be there, as active participants. It can't happen without us and nobody can do it for us" (Wheatley, 1992, p. 151).

An achievement dilemma created the need for Northview to use and share information with one another. Seventy students at Highlands Middle School and ninety students at Northview High School were found to be seriously deficient in their reading. Before spending money on a remediation plan, district leadership asked the school improvement teams to find out why these students were delayed readers. The majority of these students had been in Northview from their early elementary grades. Staff was surprised to discover that these were long term North-view students. They had assumed these low performing students had transferred into the district.

The ensuing search for answers was an arduous process involving weeks of cumulative file review. The school improvement teams found two reasons for the delayed reading skills: low attendance and poor vocabulary development. These reasons for reading problems conflicted with staff's recommended remediation plan. District leadership processed this critical discrepancy with school improve-ment teams. Many staff asked, "Is there a practical way to manage a large amount of student data and to make sense of it?" In response, the district sought a data management system that would gather a broad range of student data and present it in a meaningful way.

At the same time a commission at the state level studied the correlation between high school student achievement and job readiness. Their research evidenced the need to drastically improve students' skills for success in a 21st century job market. Northview implemented a data management system to more closely monitor student progress and career readiness skills. This constituted a major shift in practice, moving from intuition to the use of data by all staff.

The following letter from the superintendent reinforced the understanding of the power of data to increase student achievement. This letter honestly shares potential challenges and benefits of using data while assuring support. It also conveys a respect for staff and their need for time to assimilate the learning. He compared the change process to the feelings Orville and Wilbur Wright must have had on that windy morning in Kitty Hawk when they took their first trial flight. Just like the Wright Brothers, Stearns went on to say, "While we may be nervous, our work will certainly change the future!" Relating change work to the pioneering effort of the Wright Brothers encouraged staff in using data to improve instruction.

AN OPEN LETTER TO STAFF FROM THE SUPERINTENDENT

Dear Staff,

   Did you ever wonder what it must have been like on that windy day at Kitty Hawk, when Wilbur and Orville finally got that plane to lift off the ground? What must have gone through their minds? I think they must have had incredible butterflies in their stomach and been wildly wide-eyed. "We did it!" I must tell you that as I have learned more about the data warehouse, I have thought about those two men who so profoundly changed the future. My emotions have run the gamut from being confused and wide-eyed to "we can do this!" After my first training on the actual software, I was excited beyond belief about the power of this product. I believe it will become an incredible tool for teachers and ultimately benefit the lives of our students.

   What have I learned so far?

1. Information is truly power. With just a few keystrokes you can start your class in the fall knowing reading levels and learning styles of all of your students—a process I have seen teachers spend hours pouring over cumulative files to generate that information.
2. Teams, departments, and grade level teachers can develop questions about the students they serve and gather insight from the software's ability to compare and contrast data.
3. We are just getting started. A lot of training and time interacting with the software will be necessary for staff to realize its full potential. We must respect every individual staff member's level of skill as we learn to use the data warehouse. We have taken recommendations from our Curriculum Council, NCA Chairpersons and technology committee to help design training for this project.
4. Support staff will be needed! I realize that support staff in the technical and data analysis areas will be needed to help teachers learn what questions to ask and how to get the software to respond to those questions.
5. Updated hardware will be needed. This is a solution we are closing in on and hope to have those solutions implemented before you all come back in the fall.
6. We must always keep our eyes on what is best for students. If by use of the data warehouse you have information that makes you better able to meet the needs of your students, then we have gone to great lengths in the service of our students.
7. Let's work together to design a preferred future! Like any other teacher tool, the data warehouse will be used in a great variety of ways by different staff. Even knowing this, I am deeply committed to the notion that implementation of the data warehouse is key to helping teachers meet the needs of a diverse student body in the future.
8. We are taking teacher input in many ways on the training sequence for implementing the data warehouse. This summer 2 teacher representatives from each building will be given in-depth training in the use of the data warehouse.
9. We plan to have some results in your hands in the fall that you can use for your class/es and that will show the power of the data warehouse.
10. Like Orville and Wilbur, we know we are going to impact the future with this work and while we may be wide-eyed and a little nervous, our preferred future is what you and I can make it. Let's take flight!

Yours for kids,

Michael A. Stearns

Michael A. Stearns, Superintendent
May 2002

The district developed a metaphor, FLIGHT! to signify the change to data-based decision making for instructional improvement. Metaphors often build a bridge from the known to the unknown, from the familiar to the unfamiliar. The power of the FLIGHT! metaphor was to give staff confidence that using data would result in improved instruction.

Student Art Work by Megan W.

Information from Outside Sources

CRITICAL FRIENDSHIP WITH TRUSTED PARTNERS

The Ball Foundation provided a new type of relationship to Northview. Their support was provided in the role of a critical friend. While it took time for this partnership to evolve, it soon became a valued resource to the district. There were some bumps along the way. Never in the history of the district had administrators been asked to examine their practice so deeply. As a matter of fact, the administrative team jokingly referred to partnership meetings as "deep-thought hell."

Suspecting we were onto something important, we prevailed through intense conversations. Ball's representative, Brayman, challenged the district to ground itself in authentic practice. It was only when we translated theory into action that the value of the partnership became clear. The Northview staff went from saying, "Oh no, not them again," to asking for input from the foundation who was now viewed as a critical friend. Critical friends are first and foremost good listeners. They listen without judgment and respond by asking probing questions that encourage self-reflection.

CRITICAL FRIENDSHIP WITH EXTERNAL COLLEAGUES

Airlines, like many businesses, employ a tagline to capture our attention. Here are a few:

> Southwest: "Stop Searching. Start Traveling."
> United: "It's time to fly."
> American: "We know why you fly."

A slogan for *Taking Flight to Literacy and Leadership!* might be, "Everyone a leader through shared learning." The emphasis on *everyone* is extraordinarily important. We have extolled the advantages of fields of learning, of collaborative learning, of processes for learning, all within the school system itself. However, for our learning to be robust for the long term we needed to cultivate learning partners outside our system.

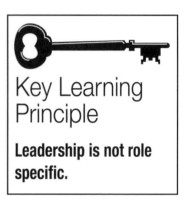

Key Learning Principle

Leadership is not role specific.

The information base of a district staff that experiences little turnover is finite. In order to build the capacity for double loop or innovative learning we need an ongoing source of dissonant information. Additionally, one of a school system's responsibilities is to share its information for the betterment of others.

Senge (1994, p. 6) admonishes us that "No single organization has the resources to conduct all the necessary experiments on its own; managers seek avidly to learn about each others' attempts, results, and reflections." School systems need each other. They all have expertise on some aspect of "what works." By connecting at the "watering hole" or in professional learning communities, they can distribute their intellectual resources and influence the professional field. By collaborating, systems can nourish and sustain each other.

According to Fullan, Hill, and Crévola in their book, *Breakthrough* (2006, p. 97), "Very small districts must form learning relationships with other districts. Larger ones must subdivide into clusters, being careful that clusters do not become isolated." They suggest that each school system is obligated to be an active participant in a broad learning community wherein they learn from other districts as well as contribute to their development. In this way the best ideas are shared widely to the advantage of all.

Our society values competition. Few question the value of getting ahead. However, getting ahead is usually won at leaving someone behind. We cannot ascribe to this mentality in the education of our children. All children can learn, and we are smart enough to figure out how to teach them. However, it is a challenge so complex we cannot do it alone.

In Kent County, Michigan, curriculum and instructional leaders banded together to share their resources, especially intellectual, to maximize the achievement of their combined population of 140,000 students. This intentional collaboration gradually stimulated a massive shift in the culture of the county's educational system.

About the same time the twenty-two superintendents developed an "all kids" mindset. They organized their meetings around learning with and supporting one another. In so doing the boundaries of their respective districts began to blur. This gave rise to new opportunities for collaboration and led to numerous fiscal efficiencies that no one had ever fathomed.

These leaders became models for their own staffs. County-wide learning groups sprang up for principals, curriculum directors, special education directors, technology leaders, and financial officers. Gradually even personnel directors, early childhood directors, and communications directors organized their own networks. The groups shared their learning (incremental learning) and eventually developed the trust necessary to create new knowledge (innovative learning) together.

The creative solutions that ensued had no limit. To date these county collaborators have developed:

- innovative policy changes

- novel partnerships with business, non-profit, and higher education communities

- a county-wide data warehouse and school improvement services

- principal recruitment processes and principal leadership academies

- a web-based curriculum in all four core content areas that is aligned to new national standards

- a county-wide study of change leadership for staff and administrators

- a network of early childhood services

- co-ordination of grassroots educational advocacy

- shared assessment development software

- a county-wide data management system

- county-wide diversity initiatives that engage students as well as staff

- a county-wide literacy coaching network

Key Learning Principle

Often we need to go slow to go fast.

To its credit, Kent Intermediate School District (KISD), the county educational service center, took responsibility to facilitate these efforts, no small task. Initially it was like herding cats with as many agendas as there were participants. Participants embraced the idea that the entire student population of the county was the responsibility of them all. This vision replaced the competition between districts with a commitment to share information and resources to promote the learning of all students.

Kevin Konarska, Kent Intermediate School District (Kent ISD) Superintendent, speaks to the value of sharing information across district borders. "Kent Intermediate Superintendents' Association chose literacy as an initiative because of its impact in the classroom to increase student achievement. Strong literacy skills lead to success in the classroom and to quality throughout one's life. We want to raise the level of importance of literacy as well as help unify our school districts and community around this important work. Working collaboratively gives it great strength. Kent ISD's role is to bring staff together to engage in learning around 'best practices,' and create an ongoing dialogue that will build the capacity of our staff to sustain this work through all districts" (Konarska, 2008, p. 1).

It is in this context that Northview took its place on the runway. In this county setting, the fuel for learning was ever abundant with county colleagues sharing information with one another and cheering on the sidelines, "Take FLIGHT! Take FLIGHT!"

Staff Conversations

A Conversation with Superintendent Stearns:

Change is the Story

"There is a connection between leadership and change," noted Stearns. "Much like a pilot who skillfully flies through turbulence, a school leader must anticipate the challenges of change in pursuit of its mission." To the superintendent of Northview, "change" was the big story.

The superintendent asked the staff to move forward with the data efforts and eventually with data-driven literacy instruction. He communicated that change was imperative in order to improve instruction and demonstrated how data was key to taking student learning to a new level. Stearns cautioned that change would be difficult. He and his leadership team listened to teachers' concerns. They provided the tools and training teachers requested and encouraged teachers to support one another. Stearns and the administrative team understood that in order to ultimately serve students, the data system needed to serve the teachers well first.

From Wheatley's work (1999) Northview recognized that changing the school system required that:

1. Understanding the change process is essential to leading and making change.

2. Information fuels learning; data is a powerful source of information for instructional planning.

3. We seek information from outside sources who can provoke our thinking and add to our knowledge.

Change challenges us to remain open to societal demands while doggedly pursuing our vision. The three strategies for change, explained in this chapter, enable us to do so. We are proactive in guiding the change process when we *honor what we know about change, use data for decision making, and gather information from critical friends and external sources.*

Key Learning Principle

Sometimes we have to try something before it makes sense.

When the weather changes in FLIGHT!, our pilot gathers information about current weather patterns in the FLIGHT! path. Using what he knows about the implication of these conditions and engaging the participation of air traffic controllers, he may choose to change the path of travel to another considerably different from the original. This change may require adaptation: more FLIGHT! time, more paperwork, more fuel, more pilot effort. However, by intentionally applying strategies for change, our pilot ensures that passengers will get to their destination—safely.

"Take-Aways"

• *What is the advantage of listening to the detractors of change initiatives?*

• *What kinds of data will fuel our learning about instructional practice?*

• *Who do we know from outside our school system who can stretch our thinking?*

Chapter 13

Culture

Tough Question:

- What is the standard for "how we do things around here"?

Key Learning Principles:

- Build on assets.
- Operate from a mindset of what is working.
- Hold high expectations for adult learning.
- Positive relationships foster learning.

Main Ideas:

- An asset-based mindset is a continual source of energy for the work.
- High expectations are essential to change, improvement and professional growth.
- Quality relationships greatly impact the success of students, staff and the school system.

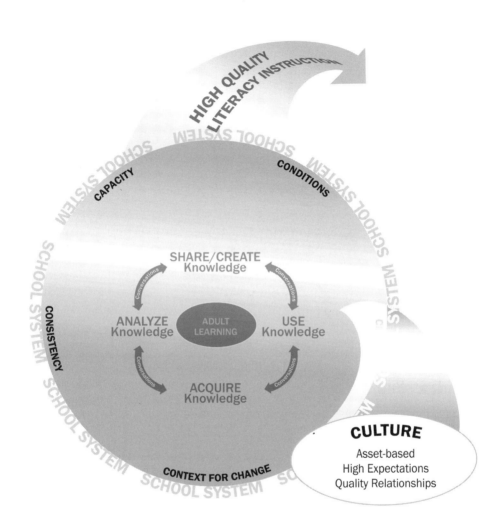

*D*efinition: *Culture is the shared values and beliefs that guide behaviors and determine the way things are done around here (Sergiovanni, 1984).*

Culture is a prime determinant in how both students and teachers learn, how teachers teach, and in how leadership and the quality of relationships are defined.

The culture of a school system is a prime determinant in how both students and teachers approach their learning. It impacts how teachers view their place in the school, the system, and community. It sets standards for how all the stakeholders interact with one another.

Schein in the 1985 text *Organizational Culture and Leadership* (as cited in Yukl, 1989) defines culture as the basic assumptions, values, and beliefs shared by members of a group or organization. These understandings reflect the group's world view and their place in it. According to Hodgkinson (1991), our values are the source of attitude, "the interface of skin and world," which in turn gives rise to behavior and action. Culture establishes norms for how our common set of assumptions, values, and beliefs are to play out within the context of the organization. In essence, culture determines our behavior in our group setting and the relationships group members will have with one another.

Leaders intentionally embed cultural standards throughout their organization with their own behavior. Schein (as cited in Yukl, 1989) suggests multiple methods of communicating cultural expectations to members.

Primary Behaviors for Establishing Culture	Secondary Behaviors for Establishing Culture
Attention: What we ask about, talk about, reinforce, and critique communicates a value of what is important.	Design of organization structure: How the organization is structured determines in what ways the members can interact, a strong statement of beliefs and values.
Reactions to Crises: Responses to dilemmas are value laden and set a precedent for how to behave in future like-situations.	Design of procedures: Guidelines for how the work gets done is evidence of values about who should do the work, how, with whom, with what resources, and with what level of autonomy.
Role Modeling: Consistent leadership behavior sets expectations for the behavior of the group.	Stories, legends and myths: Stories exemplify tradition and expectations. They suggest what is important to the organization both in the past and for the future.
Allocation of Rewards: Promotions and formal recognition communicate what is valued by the leader and encourages the targeted behavior.	Formal statements: Occasional formal statements are a supplement to a leader's ongoing communication and behavior. To have impact on development of culture, they need to align tightly to the leader's words and actions.
Criteria for selection and dismissal: Recruitment of people with particular skills or traits as well as their promotion reflects the leaders values.	Design of facilities: The physical layout of a facility can reflect a commitment to openness and inclusivity or to tight control and limited access to one another.

The culture of a school system is a prime determinant in how both students and teacher approach their learning. It impacts how teachers view their place in their school, the system, and community. It sets standards for how all the stakeholders interact with one another.

Northview employed three highly value-laden strategies to promote the culture of learning and quality relationships.

Culture's Strategies:

- Build On Assets

- Set High Expectations

- Foster Quality Relationships between All Groups

Build on Assets

When staff is in the midst of change, they must be mindful of the essence of who they are as individuals, what they are collectively, and where they are headed. It is essential that staff understands what their strengths are. It is knowledge of these strengths that gives them the foundation to make needed changes.

The asset-based mindset of the Northview central office staff supplied ongoing energy for the staff. No matter where the superintendent and his assistants spoke, they framed the conversation in terms of "what was possible" given the knowledge, skills, and commitment of the staff. These central office administrators delivered an intentional, consistent message of high regard for the staff and their ability to do whatever it took to increase the achievement of all students. "Yes," these leaders would say, "overcoming this hurdle won't be easy, but together, we can do this given our many strengths."

This asset-based mindset aligns tightly with the principles of a process called appreciative inquiry. Appreciative inquiry was developed in the 1980's by David Cooperrider. He found that when he asked questions that were problem focused, people lost energy and became less engaged with the interview. However, when he asked about why things succeeded, the interviewees' level of interest and energy increased (Preskill, Torres, Piontek, 2006).

Key Learning Principle

Build on assets.

Cooperrider (2000) and his colleagues who coined the term "Appreciative Inquiry" developed principles for this technique. Three of these principles are applicable to the asset-based mindset of Northview's administrators.

1. The Anticipatory Principle: the most important resources we have for change are our collective imagination and our conversations about the future. Our image of the future provides a roadmap to guide us. The more positive and hopeful the image, the more positive the action.

2. The Positive Principle: Change requires positive attitudes such as hope, inspiration, and the joy of creating with one another. People move in the direction of their inquiries—positive mindsets result in positive action.

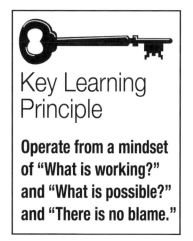

Key Learning Principle

Operate from a mindset of "What is working?" and "What is possible?" and "There is no blame."

3. The Enactment Principle: To really make a change, we must be the change we want to see. Positive change occurs when we have a model of the ideal future. We must live the way we want to be. We create the future with our words, images, and relationships.

Hammond and Hall (1998, pp. 20-21) spin Appreciative Inquiry principles slightly differently:

- In every organization, something works.

- What we focus on becomes our reality.

- Reality is created in the moment, and there are multiple realities.

- The language we use creates our reality.

By publicly recognizing the staff's assets and designating them as the foundation of future work, the Northview central office team lit a fire of collective confidence. As confidence was built, staff was more willing to assume responsibility for not only determining their own needs for literacy learning, but also to step up to the plate and teach one another.

Northview's administrative team seized opportunities to build upon staff's assets to foster instructional improvement.

Staff Conversations

A Conversation with Administrative Team Members:

Build On Strengths

Dan Duba, Highlands Middle School principal, sees himself as a servant to the staff. He says, "I have an effective staff. They know that we will work together on anything they need to foster learning for each and every student. They believe that it's not a matter of yes or no but of what we need to do for students. We work together when it comes to student learning."

Mark Thomas, Northview High School principal, adds, "I want to build on what my staff uses to be the best they can be. I want part of my story to be on asking great questions that motivate us to think about why we use the practices we do. We need to know that our instructional practices are best practices and research-supported. Staff members use their data, and offer their best thinking and solutions. They are empowered to lead the way to improvement."

Tricia Hampel, West Oakview Elementary principal, comments, "Our staff wants to learn and draw on each others' knowledge. We really work to foster that. It requires that we are all good listeners and share abundantly what we know. That way we will always have a source of information for learning."

Set High Expectations

When we board a plane, it goes without saying that we hold high expectations for arriving safely and on time. Over time the public's expectations for excellent customer service from airlines have diminished. Conversely, for school staff, expectations continually climb.

What are "high expectations"? Northview developed a culture of high expectations defined by:

- Collective Efficacy
- Expectational Learning

COLLECTIVE EFFICACY

"I've led schools for many years. I've learned that teachers solve problems best when they themselves identify areas where change is needed and when they develop solutions. Even if I have what I consider a great insight, the whole faculty must embrace the ideas if it's going to go anywhere" (Hoerr, 2009, p. 80).

When teachers believe that there are benefits to collegiality which lead to increased student learning, it sets the stage for collaborative practice. As new opportunities surface and teachers utilize the knowledge of their colleagues, they create better ideas and solutions while gaining respect, confidence, and competency.

Anne Jolly (2008, p. 3) describes what she terms, "joint work." "When groups of teachers work together as interdependent colleagues and rigorously examine together teaching and learning, they are engaging in mature, collaborative work. In this type of collaboration, teachers learn together. They jointly develop and coordinate their instructional practices. Teachers develop a collective sense of responsibility for the students they teach. When this type of collaboration occurs school wide, the school becomes a professional learning community in the truest sense." Collective efficacy is a state of mind. It is achieved when staff collaborates on work that leads to high levels of learning.

Teachers in collaborative learning teams influence and can transform each others' practice. Describing the "best kind of learning," Chappuis, Chappuis, and

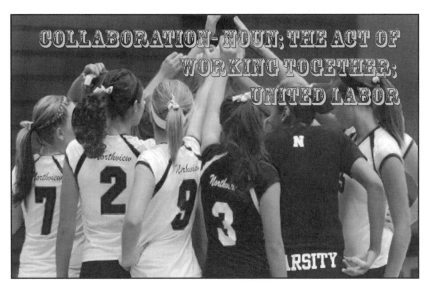

Student Art Work by Kelley W.

Stiggins (2009, p. 60) relate, "Collaborative learning teams provide more than one-time exposure to new ideas. Over time, they can change day-to-day teaching by giving teachers the ongoing opportunity to learn together, apply learning to the classroom, and reflect on what works and why. Just as learning improves for students when they have the structured opportunity to reflect on what they know and don't know in relation to the targets of instruction, adult learning also benefits from intentional reflection on classroom practice. Collaborative learning teams can transform the nature of adult interaction and learning in schools by engaging teachers in the same process of continual learning and improvement that we ask our students to strive for in their work."

Staff efficacy grows as they impact each others' instructional practice and observe the result of increased learning and achievement.

Staff Conversations

A Conversation with Connie Petter, K-12 Learning Consultant, and Theresa Blank, Literacy Coach:

We Make a Difference with Our Colleagues

Connie Petter, district learning consultant, suggests, "We all have the potential to make a difference with our colleagues. It takes the school system encouraging sharing, collaboration, and networking. Teachers report more gratification and motivation."

Connie explains further, "The system has been intentional about motivating people to use their instructional expertise. They catch on fire to share instructional strategies with colleagues. Beyond individual contributions, the real story is about growing the individual and the school system through development of a collaborative culture."

Theresa Blank, a literacy coach, adds, "We have tried on the new clothes of collaboration; it feels so rewarding. We see the effect of modeling lessons and giving teachers the opportunity to learn with and from each other. Our data is showing that it is making a difference as we lead and learn together."

EXPECTATIONAL LEARNING

Another facet of developing high expectations for staff was a shift in the school system's view of "professional development." It was a subtle change from inviting staff to learn about specific programs to expecting them to learn continually about their students' needs and how best to meet them.

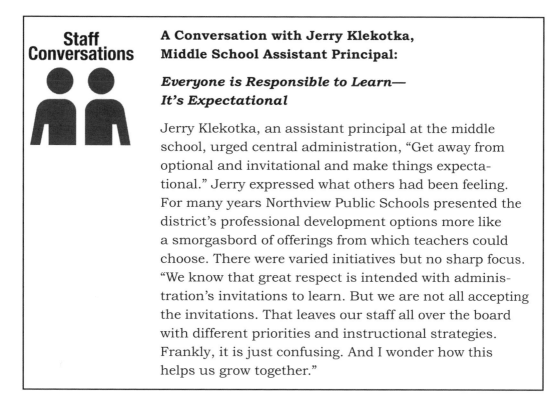

Staff Conversations

A Conversation with Jerry Klekotka, Middle School Assistant Principal:

Everyone is Responsible to Learn— It's Expectational

Jerry Klekotka, an assistant principal at the middle school, urged central administration, "Get away from optional and invitational and make things expectational." Jerry expressed what others had been feeling. For many years Northview Public Schools presented the district's professional development options more like a smorgasbord of offerings from which teachers could choose. There were varied initiatives but no sharp focus. "We know that great respect is intended with administration's invitations to learn. But we are not all accepting the invitations. That leaves our staff all over the board with different priorities and instructional strategies. Frankly, it is just confusing. And I wonder how this helps us grow together."

Teachers longed for direction. They were willing to participate but wanted clear signals as to what the expectations were. Accordingly, the school system worked in novel ways to accommodate teachers' need to learn consistent strategies for instruction. Initially only small amounts of time appeared to be available for staffs' learning. However, once staff was involved in helping to design a schedule for their learning, they generated new solutions. They were able to schedule regular chunks of time for professional development. This reinforced the belief that:

- we all are learners all the time;
- we are responsible to ensure that all of our students are learning well; thus, we need to be teaching well;
- we focus our conversations on the critical issue of student learning.

Foster Quality Relationships Between All Groups

QUALITY RELATIONSHIPS: TEACHER TO TEACHER

Look around you on this FLIGHT! How connected do you feel to your fellow passengers? Perhaps you choose to capture some reading time or a much needed snooze. Or perhaps you would rather strike up a conversation with a seatmate. Likewise, our relationships with our peers are a matter of choice; we determine how we interact with others. These choices can make or break the success of our students, ourselves, and our school system.

Quality professional relationships can impact student achievement. It follows that:

- since student achievement is highly correlated to our instructional effectiveness,

- and since instructional effectiveness is impacted by learning new information about our practice,

- and since information is shared through our interactions with one another,

- then, our relationships need to be in very good condition to maximize the exchange of information and its impact on improving our instruction,

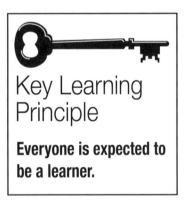

Key Learning Principle

Everyone is expected to be a learner.

- which is a key predictor in student achievement.

Quality relationships are determined by three key factors:

1. Sharing a common, compelling mission: In Northview "Preparing Students for Life's Next Step" resonated across the entire K-12 system. All staff understood its meaning.

2. Working well together: The PLC process gave a format to teachers sharing information and instructional techniques. One fifth grade teacher commented, "We have the opportunity to come together every day, share strategies, and we are so much more effective instructionally."

3. Trusting one another: Trusting one another contributes to building a common vision. It was in trusting relationships that Northview rallied support for its common purpose, establishment of a razor-sharp focus on literacy.

A school system can intentionally promote trust to increase quality relationships. Trust is essential to strong human ties and a healthy community. By virtue of our human condition, we all need and want to trust. Studies suggest that we are neurologically programmed to trust. What is trust? According to Paxton and Smith (*The Greater Good*, 2008, p. 15), "Trust is defined as the expectation that other people's future actions will safeguard our interests. It is the magic ingredient that makes our social life possible. . . . We trust others when we take a chance, yielding them some control over our money, secrets, safety, or other things we value."

Trust enables positive interaction between individuals. A lack of trust limits free flow of interaction and learning in community. Interestingly, a factor in the development of trust is how much contact people have with other people. People who belong to groups have increased interaction and tend to become more trusting as a result. The science of trust purports that the more groups we belong to—and it makes little difference what the group is—the more trust we enjoy.

Consider the implications for the school system when it builds trusting relationships. For example:

- when the system establishes structures for staff to meet regularly, (such as PLC's),

- when the leadership interacts with staff regularly,

- when super-hubs and coaches are available to support their peers,

then, staff trusts one another and the quality of their interaction improves. Opportunities to learn from one another flourish.

QUALITY RELATIONSHIPS: STUDENT TO TEACHER

Relationship building between students and teachers is critical to student success. Richard DuFour and Robert Eaker (1998) state, "It is only when students feel a connection to their teachers—when students believe that they are recognized, respected, and valued—that teachers are in a position to make a difference in students' lives" (p. 281).

Gail Boushey and Joan Moser (2006), literacy experts, convey an understanding of trust as an essential foundation for literacy learning. In their book, *The Daily Five*, they offer, "We believe positive relationships are the first and most vital element of our children's learning process. Meaningful learning requires respect between the teacher and students as well as the students themselves. We treat children as valuable individuals, each one unique and worthy of respect and caring . . . taking the time to build trust and demonstrate caring is the foundation upon which all other elements of our literacy learning are built" (p. 18).

Little did we know how data had the power to cultivate trust and respect while enhancing relationships between students and teachers. Having real time data at teachers' fingertips allowed students and teachers to assess students' academic progress on a daily basis. The data provided an objective, common connection around which students and teachers could develop a relationship. Because teachers knew more about students, and students had access to their own data, they could confer with one another to support, celebrate, or problem solve.

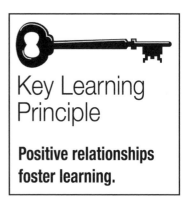

Key Learning Principle

Positive relationships foster learning.

Students' academic programs no longer belonged solely to the school. Their data was a numerical story of their education over which they now had access, input, and control. Certainly teachers stood ready to support students through tutoring and guidance. More importantly, students could see that they were in charge of their own "next steps." Students and teachers now jointly owned the responsibility for student success.

Staff Conversations

A Conversation with Dan Matthews, High School Assistant Principal:

Building Relationships and Connecting with Kids

Dan Matthews, Assistant Principal at Northview High School, states, "Through the FLIGHTS! program, we are able to do an excellent job knowing our students' needs. We can help them in a more targeted way. It helps us serve students to be successful, helps us build quality relationships, and helps us interact and work more effectively with families as they support their kids. We are able to serve students in a timelier manner."

Dan checks the FLIGHTS! program each morning and throughout the day. To him, it's a tool of instant opportunity. When Matthews sees a student struggling with low grades or missing assignments he calls the student down to his office or makes a classroom visit. "Hey, what's going on? What can we do to help? " He may discover absenteeism is the cause. He may find information about family, home, or friendships that are at risk, or may just find that a student doesn't know where to start or how to accomplish the task.

Matthews reaches out to make a contact each and every day with every student who is struggling. He is always out supporting students. After one-on-one conversations with students, he contacts the families and works together with them to make a plan. Dan comments, "It's funny, I would never have guessed that I would be able to develop such rich relationships with students by using data, but that's what I'm able to do. When I talk to a parent who thanks me for taking the time to call with a concern, I know we are on the right track. Kids feel we are there for them. We are all up on using the data system to help them be successful every day."

QUALITY RELATIONSHIPS: ADMINISTRATOR TO STAFF

It is often said that a school administrator's job is the loneliest job in the world. It does not have to be that way if a school system makes quality relationships a high priority. Administration can develop a cadre of colleagues who gladly stand shoulder to shoulder with them in pursuit of improved student learning. It is this shared purpose that binds administration and staff in quality relationships.

According to Senge (1990), "The world is full of teams of talented individuals who share a vision for a while, yet fail to learn. The great jazz ensemble has talent and shared vision, but what really matters is that the musicians know how to play together" (p. 236).

School teams can develop highly productive relationships that have nothing to do with personal friendships and everything to do with purpose. It is shared responsibility that binds individuals together so they can accomplish together what they cannot do alone.

The administrative team in Northview intentionally worked at forging quality relationships with their staff by:

1. recognizing student *and* teacher success,

2. creating a trusting, risk-free environment for innovation,

3. fostering a caring, welcoming environment, and

4. laughing and having fun.

1. Recognizing student and teacher success

According to Schmoker (1996, p. 104), "Teachers can guide themselves in many meaningful ways, but principals and other leaders have a responsibility to reinforce individual and collective effort. . . . An atmosphere of acknowledgment and appreciation is essential." He also suggests that if teachers are to work well together, leaders must recognize their accomplishments.

In Northview, every Board of Education meeting began with a celebration of student accomplishment throughout the system. This sent a strong message to the staff and the community at large that we are all partners in educating students. Student success is our success. From academic achievement to the arts to the playing field, student accomplishments were highly publicized. Publicly recognizing student achievements heightened staff's sense of shared purpose in preparing students to "fly." According to Blasé and Kirby (1992) attempts to publicly recognize quality efforts can make a significant difference in improving schools.

Each month the superintendent solicited student nominations for Board of Education recognition. These nominations provided teachers a way to publicly affirm their influence on student learning. This was another expression of an asset-based culture steeped in high expectations.

To encourage staff and student reflection on the school system's mission, Stearns held an annual essay contest for high school juniors. The topic was, "What Does the Mission Statement 'Preparing Students for Life's Next Step' Mean to Me?" The winner of the contest was invited to read his essay at the kick-off ceremony for the school year. Historically Northview had hired nationally known speakers to inspire teachers. But hearing a student share the meaning of a Northview education profoundly affected staff. Not only was it a confirmation of what students could do, it was a testament to teachers' hard work as well. An excerpt from an essay written by a Northview High School junior stands as an example of this confirmation:

"Life is an ocean full of opportunity, with new situations, challenges, and choices everyday. In terms of offering a variety of opportunities I can think of no better example than Northview. At school, students have the chance everyday to try something new, challenge themselves, and make their own decisions. The administration and staff are always there with a guiding hand to assist us in making the best decision in order to help prepare us for the future. Thanks to the staff we will have a firm grasp on the world's opportunities to help stay afloat in the big waters of life."

All these examples of recognition require little more than a bit of administrators' creativity and sincere hearts. Teachers must believe that the appreciation is genuine and not patronizing. They need to know that the recognition is an honest reflection of their relationship with their leaders.

Generally teachers seldom receive sufficient recognition for their hard work. Since the famous "A Nation at Risk Report" of 1983, teachers have been on the firing line for the inadequacies of student performance. The research of Blasé and Kirby (1992) found that most teachers have unmet needs for approval. Lortie's (1975) study found that this need for recognition has a direct influence on a school's capacity to obtain results.

Schmoker (1996, p.107) relates, "[Teachers] deserve recognition; our schools can only benefit from granting it. When deserving people are not appropriately appreciated for all they do, entropy may rush in. . . . If we frequently clarify and celebrate progress toward goals and the impact of our efforts on students, we help to sustain the conditions essential to a healthy, ever-improving workplace." Schmoker suggests that regularly reinforcing the accomplishments of the staff, both publicly and privately, is one of the most effective ways to create a focus on the shared purpose.

2. Creating a trusting, risk-free environment for innovation

When a school system understands that they need to create their own solutions to challenges, innovation becomes a primary activity for the staff. In 2000, few school districts had heard of a data warehouse, let alone possessed one. Stearns and staff recognized the potential of using technology to make data-based decisions about instruction. However, when Northview purchased their data warehouse, little did the school system know that it would not be teacher friendly, nor produce data reports in real time to guide teacher's planning. But it did not take staff long to realize the warehouse's shortcomings.

This was the superintendent's "baby." He had high hopes for its effectiveness. What was the staff to do? They confronted their boss and told him what worked and what did not. They insisted on tools that would help them improve their practice, and they requested regular training. All of this could have created much conflict between Stearns and his staff. However, he listened to staff's complaints. He opened his mind to staff's suggestions and asked, "What might be possible and what more do you need?"

Staff came to trust this open communication process, and as their trust developed, staff's willingness to use technology flourished. Senge (1990, p. 284) states that openness is a characteristic of relationships. "It is the willingness to suspend what we think in order to understand another's viewpoint. . . . If openness is a quality of relationships, then building relationships characterized by openness may be one of the most high leverage actions to build organizations characterized by openness." In our openness we seek to understand another's reality. It is a suspension of our own need for power and control. Openness makes us vulnerable and commits us to developing the capacity of others.

Stearns encouraged the idea that "we will achieve great things together" through listening and open communication as evidenced in the letter on the following page.

The development of trust works both ways. Ideally staff trusts administration and vice versa. Senge (1990) uses the metaphors of championship sports teams and great jazz ensembles for acting in coordinated ways. He states, "Outstanding teams in organizations develop the same sort of relationship—an 'operational trust,' where each team member remains conscious of the other team members and can be counted on to act in ways that complement each others' actions" (p. 236).

As part of a groundswell of effort focused upon literacy, Northview's language arts committee created a literacy leadership group which designed several innovations to guide the practices of all staff. With Grey's encouragement they designed a literacy framework that provided staff with a common vocabulary as well as a set of shared practices. In order to implement their innovations this group had to assume a leadership role. Originally they thought they were "sticking their necks out," uncertain of staff's response. However, the superintendent joined them in communicating the literacy framework to their peers at every building: "This is where we are headed. We are doing this together K-12. This is why. This is what will happen if we do not."

Dear Staff,

I would like to share an update with all of you regarding our data warehouse project. You have heard your administrative staff discussing the notion of a data warehouse, so let's begin by understanding what a data warehouse is and what it can do for staff. A data warehouse is like a big storage bin of student's cumulative records in the sky. It is capable of handling great amounts of information. We can put everything we know about students for as long as they are at NVPS on this database. Once all our student information is in the data warehouse (we currently have our first upload in the data warehouse), we can manipulate the data to provide useful information on the students in our classrooms and, based on this information, *design instruction to meet their needs*. At a simple level, with the data warehouse, a teacher can, in the fall, ask the computer for a graph of the most current reading level of his/her students. A teacher can access the learning styles of his/her students by entering a simple query. A department or grade level can determine what students have passed what standards, again with a simple computer process. A teacher at her/his PC can access trends on attendance for any student they have. This data warehouse can do much more in making comparisons, analyzing data, and providing information on individual students and entire classrooms of students.

Staff may find the following information helpful in understanding how we will implement this project:

1) No teacher will be required to enter data. The technology department will coordinate that.
2) Key staff at each building will be trained on how to access the program and how to do queries. We will then use a "trainer of trainers" model to train all staff.
3) All staff will be able to access the data warehouse from their own desktop computer.
4) The first wave of training will most likely happen in April.
5) With your input, we will be designing a set of standard queries that can be accessed from the data warehouse.
6) At a district level, the data warehouse will be used to comply with information required by the new accreditation system.
7) The data warehouse can be used for the NCA documentation process.
8) It is our intent that the data warehouse will also hold a solution for developing EDPs that will soon be required by the state.
9) The data warehouse is being funded by a combination of funds from the Ball Foundation and a state career prep grant. To keep the data warehouse up and running in the future a nominal fee based on district enrollment will be paid to the software provider.

Let's learn together! The data warehouse is a powerful tool for teachers! It can provide all kinds of information on our students. As we begin to understand this system and how to use it, we will encounter many questions. Please feel free to bring those questions forward to your building administrators. TetraData, the company that is providing our data warehouse, is extremely user friendly. They have made a commitment to work with our district to maximize the use of this great resource. All we have to do is ask!

It is the goal of the administrative staff to provide the necessary support to staff as we begin this journey. I share their commitment and am convinced this will become a great service to staff, students, and our Northview families.

Michael A. Stearns
Superintendent

The committee then trusted building administrators to support these initiatives. Accordingly principals held ongoing conversations with their staffs around the new literacy practices. They provided time for staff to learn about and experiment with them. Principals also just asked staff for their support—and the literacy strategies flourished.

When a mutual trust between staff and administration prevails, innovation, implementation and improvement can be the order of the day. Brayman relates a story of being liberated as a professional by a superior who challenged her to "push the envelope." He reassured her that he expected her to operate on the cutting edge, trying new ideas and failing. "We'll come pick you up and dust you off," he said. "We just assume you will learn from your mistakes the first time and move ahead. That way we all can profit from your efforts."

Administration builds trust by treating teachers as the professionals they are, as experts in both instruction and content. Administrators can communicate the importance of staff's work by visiting classrooms, engaging in collegial conversations, and promoting positive staff interactions with the school board and community.

Stearns and the administrative team made classroom visitation a priority by clearing their calendars to spend one full day a week in classroom visitations throughout the district. Building level staff looked forward to these visits to showcase the students' work, and simultaneously their own. The administrative team used these visits to remain informed on instructional and literacy practices. Staff did not view these visits as evaluative. Instead, teachers trusted that administrators visited as a demonstration of support and for the advancement of the school system's practices.

3.   Fostering a caring, welcoming environment

One only needs to enter the doors of a school building to sense the interpersonal energy. It permeates the air. The extent to which one feels welcomed and included influences the development of a community and its commitment. In Northview the staff highly values the way they relate to one another as well as to students, parents, and other community members. They describe themselves as warm and friendly. Stearns often received thank-you's from new parents who relate how positively they were received as they came to enroll their child.

School volunteers were always seen as integral members of the school family. They helped to support the entire schooling effort with their assistance and participation in school activities. According to Schmoker (2006) every adult affiliated with the school system needs to be valued as a resource to promote learning. "Every employee, including bus drivers and cafeteria workers, receives profound respect" (p. 71).

4. Laughing and having fun

Making quality relationships a priority acknowledges the social nature of learning. Schmoker (1996) challenges us to "consider the benefits of placing high value on humor and having fun. In Northview the superintendent often encouraged staff to be sure to not allow a day to go by without laughing. This was true even at the bargaining table when tensions ran high; humor would often save the day.

Before report cards were to go out in November, shortly after implementing a standard-based report card, Stearns received a frenzied call that all the data the teachers had entered had been lost. The lead teacher was in tears. Before addressing the distressed staff, Stearns turned to the teacher and said, "Remember, there is no crying in baseball." This brought a smile to the teacher's face. Stearns followed up with a gift of a t-shirt to the lead teacher on which the quote was printed. The teacher proudly displayed the t-shirt in her room for the rest of the year. This story made its way through the district and when a tough situation arose, you could often hear a teacher laugh and say, "Well, there is no crying in baseball."

Quality relationships create a dynamic of respect, trust, caring, and fun between administration and staff enabling a group to accomplish their shared purpose more effectively.

Fostering quality relationships is an essential ingredient of Northview's learning culture. For the adults, honoring staff's assets, working well together, and trusting one another are essential. Staff shares high expectations for professional learning. For the students, staff exemplifies and communicates the value of strong relationships in student-teacher interactions and in K-12 policies and practices. Teachers recognize the role quality relationships play in students' success.

A few hours into visiting Northview Public Schools, Myron Rogers, Ball Foundation consultant (2003) observed, "It is obvious that the school system's identity is based on quality relationships." An individual or system's identity is how it describes its own value to self, others, and the world. Not only did Rogers peg the district's identity accurately, he also discerned a major facet of its culture.

Together, quality relationships, high expectations, and an asset-based mindset establish a standard for "how things are done around here" (Sergiovanni, 1984) within the system and with external organizations. Having predictable standards creates an environment of trust. It institutionalizes norms wherein staff appreciate each others' assets and work well with one another for the sake of students. Knowing their strengths are recognized, people want to be the best they can be. This stimulates a high regard for individual and collective accomplishment. It is a culture that generates energy for learning and growing.

Do you want to book a FLIGHT! on an aircraft powered by a piston engine with propellers, or on one with jet engines? A jet engine is needed to move school systems forward to improve each and every student's achievement. An intentionally crafted culture can increase the thrust of student achievement (Marzano, Waters, and McNulty, 2005).

So, how fast do we want to go? The answer is "as fast as we possibly can."

"Take-Aways"

• *How can we define and communicate the culture of the system to all stakeholders?*

• *How can we simultaneously use both the assets and problems of our current reality to foster growth?*

• *How can we hold each other accountable to achieve high expectations and maintain quality relationships?*

Chapter 14

Conditions

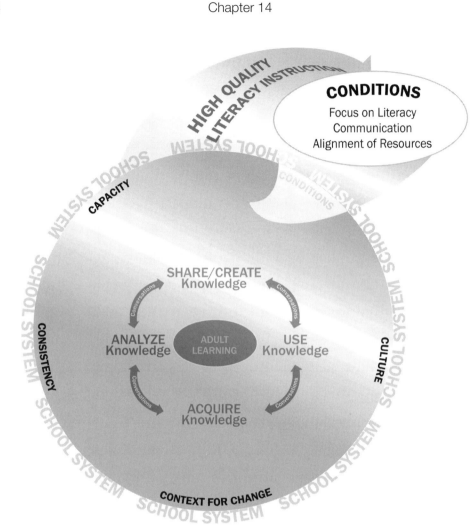

*D*efinition: *Conditions include the focus a school system chooses as its top priority, the ongoing communication used to convey and exchange information, and the tangible arrangements of time, space, and resources that influence student learning.*

Conditions' Strategies:

- Focus on Literacy

- Communication

- Alignment of Resources

Focus on Literacy

Have you ever noticed how orderly boarding a plane is? Everyone heads in the same direction in a predictable way. All passengers are focused. They have one set protocol for boarding the plane. Contrast this to asking any public school administrator to name the focus in his district, and the likely answer will be improving achievement and test scores. "If you follow up by asking which two or three strategies are being used to achieve this result, you are likely to get a puzzled look or a list of twenty discrete programs" (Wagner, Kegan, Lahey, Lemons, Garnier, Helsing, Howell, Thurber Rasmussen, 2006, p. 65).

In education we have embraced countless programs in an attempt to find "the answer" to meet student needs. This search has distracted us from creating a unified focus for our work. Most districts have multiple balls in the air which distract them from predictable, long term effort on anything.

Northview began a study of the changing demands of the 21st century workplace. The study revealed that workers need high levels of literacy, defined broadly as making and creating meaning from the written and spoken word. It stood to reason that since literacy provides the foundation for success in all academic areas and equips students with knowledge, skills, and tools for employment and citizenship, then it should be designated as the focus of the instructional effort, K-12. It was the key to "Preparing students for life's next step," the district mission. The Board of Education recognized the value of literacy to the mission of the district. Without hesitation they adjusted their goals to reflect literacy as the highest priority for the district's academic program.

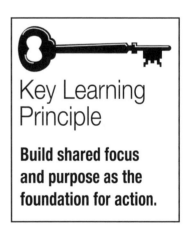

Key Learning Principle

Build shared focus and purpose as the foundation for action.

The idea of creating a district focus around literacy is certainly not a new idea; however, its power cannot be understated.

For students of *Good to Great* (Collins, 2001), establishing a district literacy focus exemplifies a key concept of transformation to greatness, the Hedgehog concept. Collins relates from Isaiah Berlin's essay, "The Hedgehog and the Fox," "The fox knows many things, but the hedgehog knows one big thing." The story goes like this.

The fox is able to devise a myriad of complex strategies for sneak attacks upon the hedgehog. Day in and out, the fox circles around the hedgehog's den, waiting for the perfect moment to pounce. Fast, sleek and beautiful, fleet of foot and crafty—the fox looks like the sure winner. The hedgehog on the other hand is a dowdier creature. He waddles along, going about his simple day, searching for lunch and taking care of his home.

The fox waits in cunning silence at the juncture in the trail. The hedgehog, minding his own business, wanders right into the path of the fox. "Aha! I've got you now!" thinks the fox. He leaps out, bounding across the ground, lightning fast. The little hedgehog, sensing danger, looks up and thinks, "Here we go again. Will he ever learn?" Rolling up in to a perfect little ball the hedgehog becomes a sphere of sharp spikes, pointing outward in all directions. The fox bounding toward his prey sees the hedgehog defense and calls off the attack. Retreating back to the forest, the fox begins to calculate the new line of attack. Each day some version of this battle between the hedgehog and the fox takes place, and despite the greater cunning of the fox, the hedgehog always wins. (Collins, p. 90-91)

What we glean from this story is the power of simplicity and focus. The unwavering success of the hedgehog belies his simple, predictable approach to life. What he intentionally employs in order to thrive is his ability to see and do what is essential and to disregard the rest. As a school district focused on literacy, Northview was able to eliminate the confusion in its daily work. The district provided everyone with the same target and the same language. A consequence of this focus was that Northview's mission statement, "Preparing students for life's next step," took on renewed meaning. Now, staff shared the same powerful strategy for getting students ready for their next step.

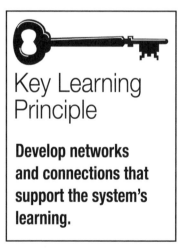

Key Learning Principle

Develop networks and connections that support the system's learning.

What became apparent was that literacy achievement was our end goal and learning about literacy instruction was our means of achieving it. Much to the relief of the entire staff, the decision was made to do one thing—literacy—and do it well throughout the district before embracing any other worthwhile goal.

Communication

When the pilot of the plane comes over the intercom, we automatically listen. We know what he has to say is important. Likewise, in a school system, we are required to communicate information so that it is readily heard and understood. Bennis and Nanus in *Leaders: The Strategies for Taking Charge* (1985), write poetically about the responsibility of leadership to communicate clear-cut messages about the organization's purpose and how it can be fulfilled. "Leaders," they say, "must relate a compelling image that fires the imagination and emotions of followers" (p. 109). This message becomes a mantra that is repeated over and over again.

What enhances the power of the message is engaging staff in the creation of the message. The more staff have a voice in determining where the organization is going, the more commitment they have to that vision (Getzels and Guba, 1954). And the message must be clear, persistent, and consistent. Staying the course by communicating a consistent and predictable desired state builds integrity and trust.

According to Fullan (2005), "High-trust cultures make the extraordinary possible, energizing people, and giving them the wherewithal to be successful under enormously demanding conditions—and giving them the confidence that staying the course will pay off" (p. 73).

So it was in Northview; the administrators were very deliberate in communicating to the staff, "This is where we are going. This is why. This is how. We can do this, no matter how hard. We do not know all the answers, but we are willing to learn with and from you. What do you think you need to get there?" They did this, over and over and over again.

When it was time to update the vision of the district, the superintendent and director of instruction went building to building, parent meeting to parent meeting, to engage stakeholders in discussions about assets and priorities for the future. After this information was processed and a literacy focus had been decided upon, back they went, building by building to clarify the new vision around the literacy focus. They spelled out its rationale, its potential for the well-being of students' current and future lives, and its challenge to the resources of the district. Questions were entertained and honored. Staff was encouraged to weigh in: "What does this mean to you and to us collectively?"

The administrative team elicited the leadership of the district literacy leadership group to communicate the potential of the literacy framework to their peers, K-12. This time the communicators were not just the leaders at the very top pointing the way, but the staff themselves disseminating the message to one another. Now the direction of the district truly belonged to everyone. No longer was central office singularly mapping the FLIGHT! of the district; instead, the practitioners themselves shared the cockpit and spoke with power and authority, peer to peer. Initially, the literacy team leaders were reticent and uncomfortable with this new role but how quickly their shyness disappeared. They knew the direction of the district; they had helped create it, and soon they were proud to help communicate and grow it.

How can we communicate with one another at every level so that knowledge can be newly created and shared? Although it is incumbent upon district leaders to communicate regularly within the district, the fact remains that few staff members have direct, frequent access to them. The reality is most staff turn to a well-informed peer to seek information and learn important skills. Most of us in the profession admit to learning the most meaningful professional information from our peers.

Key Learning Principle

Communicate your shared purpose consistently and persistently.

Doug Reeves (2006, p. 47) calls these information-rich staff members, "super hubs." With our colleagues, our learning is automatically job-embedded, informal, just-in-time, and non-evaluative. That kind of information source is accessible and risk-free. According to Ricci and Rogers (2003), the learning that gets transferred is about what works and what doesn't. It moves to a community of common practitioners via subtle informal networks and tacit interactions.

In Northview, central office administrators recognized the existence of staff members who served as super hubs to their colleagues. These hubs became catalysts for supporting teachers' quest for improving their instructional practice. Building principals created time and space for peer-to-peer modeling and coaching.

Reeves (2006, p. 48) proposes that "Understanding, identifying, and deploying networks for positive results is the central challenge of leaders who seek to transform the status quo. Rather than trying to contrive networks through organizational charts or rigid hierarchies, school leaders should harness the power of the networks that they already have by listening to their key members—which is the greatest leadership technique of all."

Leaders ask themselves, "How can I leverage connections to the super hubs?" The tighter the communication link between the formal leader and super hubs, the better. This takes time and intentional effort. The payoff comes in making key information available to the entire staff.

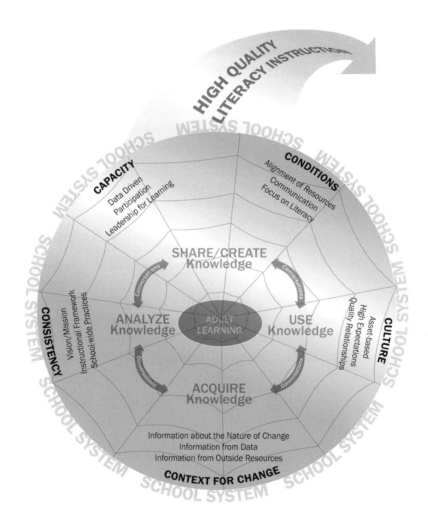

A network is like a spiderweb of communication with all staff connected across the system.

Staff Conversations

A Conversation with Super Hub, Karen Aupperlee, Literacy Leader:

Staff Come to Me

Karen Aupperlee, an elementary literacy coach, conveys a humble attitude as she reflects on the many ways she approaches her literacy coaching role. "It is rewarding to be in a position to work with staff and serve their needs in literacy instruction. I can help colleagues who request it. I share with them, and they share with me. I think it's a win-win!"

Staff members gravitate to her as a resource and partner. She values staff and builds upon a sense of what Donald A. McAndrew calls, "an assumption of competence" (2005, p. 94). He states, "Trust and the potential for nurturing it, require not only that literacy leaders make the assumption of competence about their students, colleagues, and community but also that this trust and assumption of competence are mutual."

Further he states, "In organizations where trust reigns, literacy leaders accept the expertise and views of others just as others accept those of the leader. Everyone involved feels a sense of satisfaction because they all are welcomed to join the enterprise as real players. Work actually becomes easier because of the willingness to share ideas and contribute to get the work done" (p. 95).

Aupperlee's role finds her networking with staff, sharing data and research, demonstrating strategies in classrooms, and coaching teachers. She is seen as an instructional resource to grow the literacy work at the school and throughout the system.

Teacher-to-teacher communication became the norm and many staff members volunteered to demonstrate strategies to their colleagues. The more staff tapped into each others' expertise, the better they became at their own instructional practice and the more confidence they developed. The teacher network of communication could be described as "reaching out to get help, then reaching out to give it."

Alignment of Resources

When gas prices went up four years ago, most airlines suffered financial setbacks. They were so fiscally compromised that their very existence was at risk. But they knew what business they were in: carrying passengers. In order to stay in business, they trimmed back on customer services, personnel, benefits, flight routes, and orders for new planes. Airlines all became masters of the "no frills" FLIGHT! What resources they have were committed to hauling passengers on key routes with limited service. Yes, we all may miss our in-flight meals and attentive service, but we still are able to hop around the country and beyond with relative efficiency and affordability. Airlines were forced to practice a "disciplined alignment" wherein they committed their resources to support the key function of their organization. With some exceptions most airlines were able to keep flying.

So, too, in school systems we need to practice intentional alignment of resources. This is truly the embodiment of "putting our treasure where our mouth is." Treasure is not only our money but all the resources we have available that can promote attainment of the vision, including:

- Time

- Staff expertise and energy

- Materials

- Training

The K-12 literacy focus in Northview was a shift in how to do business. It necessitated system-wide analysis of resource allocation to answer the question, "Are district resources of time, energy, learning opportunities, and revenues aligned with our focus on literacy?"

We clarified our purposes, examined our strategies, and revamped the school system's budget to ensure that we could deliver a curriculum rich in quality literacy instruction. The following chart explains how resources were aligned to support literacy.

Key Learning Principle

Trust allows staff to try new ideas and fail, as well as speak truthfully without fear of reprisal.

Resource Alignment for Literacy	
Alignment of Resources	**Impact**
Field of Work: Literacy • Classroom libraries were funded by being tagged as priority items by administration. • Literacy leaders made presentations to the Board of Education. • Teachers made selections of books and district curriculum office ordered and distributed materials. Local and national bookstores made donations. • The community was invited to donate titles to classrooms and building libraries. • Funds for learning specific literacy strategies were provided. Principals and literacy leadership group planned professional development at varied times—over the summer, after school, prior to the opening of school in the fall, during staff meetings, etc. • Professional development venues were creatively identified such as local coffee shops, teachers' homes, libraries, visitations to other classrooms within and across buildings. • A literacy coach network was established. • Area university professors and Kent Intermediate School Literacy Leaders obtained grant funding to establish a literacy coaching network at the county level. • Northview's Superintendent and Director of Instruction prioritized their district's support for its own literacy coaches. • Interested teachers could apply to be literacy coaches. An expertise with literacy strategies, adult learning, and leadership skills were required for application. • Initially, three literacy coaches were identified and received training at Kent Intermediate School District, along with other literacy leaders sent by their respective school districts. • Literacy materials were purchased for school and home use. Northview's Educational Foundation supported the initiative by providing funds. • Professional references were purchased for staff book clubs. Staff members suggested titles for purchase. Building literacy leaders coordinated, organized, and implemented the suggestions. • A local book store and publisher's representatives offered discounts for multiple copy purchases. Building principals supported the initiative as monies became available during the school year. • Teachers expanded their own professional libraries as they were able to keep copies of books purchased by the district. • Student teachers were also able to participate in these staff book clubs.	• Students K-12 have literacy materials to support their learning. • All teachers K-12 had the support materials to become teachers of literacy. • Teachers were supported in their learning with the help of coaches and peers.

Alignment of Resources	Impact
Field of Work: Adult Learning • Staff meeting times were allocated for professional learning. • Administrators sought to minimize the administrivia, communicated more via technology, and thus, devoted more of their regular staff meeting time to literacy and professional learning. Often teachers were surveyed on specific topics they wished to focus upon. • Teachers in many buildings often were responsible for volunteering to share expertise with colleagues during these staff meeting times. • Contractual agreements with the education association redesigned time for professional learning. • Staff at all levels designed creative ways to capture additional time for professional learning and collaboration. • Teachers partnered in creating opportunities to network and collaborate. • Time was provided to meet with peers, model lessons, and hold professional conversations. • Principals made the effort to obtain "rotating subs" that covered different teachers to work with colleagues for a period(s) during the day. • Work on literacy strategies, curriculum alignment, and data analyses are examples of some of the purposes of collaborative meetings.	• Teachers increased instructional expertise. • Professional learning became "expectational" and job-embedded. • Conversation became the key vehicle for learning. • Peers began to teach and learn from one another.
Field of Work: Systems Work • The literacy focus was communicated as a priority to attaining vision and mission. The Board of Education, district committees, and all staff established literacy goals. • The Board of Education endorsed the literacy focus as the primary work of the district. • Literacy leaders keep the literacy focus alive by posting displays of literacy initiatives in the district office, site of Board of Education public meetings. • Uninterrupted literacy instruction was scheduled and designed by staff. • Volunteers from any content area could participate with the building principal in helping to design the schedule to best meet students' needs. • Staff received training with skills to use their data to plan instruction.	• The entire district and community understood literacy as its top priority. • The entire staff shared common vocabulary and practices. • The school system work became streamlined and easier to understand.

Alignment of Resources	Impact
Systems Work, continued • A Data Diggers Group, charged with assisting their colleagues with understanding and interpreting data, was formed. This group received a small stipend for their additional duties. • Principals, the Director of Instruction, learning consultants, and literacy and technology leaders helped with the efforts to help teachers use their data to plan instruction and interventions. • All staff's participation was encouraged and expected. • Communications from the district office, principals, department heads, literacy leaders, and others reinforced the power of a singular focus on literacy. • A plan for system-wide consistency was developed. Conversations were at the heart of the effort to be consistent. • Administrative conversations occurred to help clarify understandings. Literacy leaders echoed the same message of and worked in partnership with administrators to support their colleagues. • Common school-wide strategies were selected by staff based upon data and student needs. • Parents and the community were engaged. Frequent communication continually reinforced the focus.	• Staff used their data to improve instruction and enhance relationships with students, families, and each other. • Staff took leadership roles at building and school system levels. • Staff began to anticipate change and develop adaptive solutions.

Alignment of resources to literacy is exemplified by the school system's purchasing recommended materials. So often materials are suggested at trainings but left to the teacher's initiative to order and pay for them. If we are serious about teachers using a recommended book or DVD, then providing it is vital to ensure their follow-up application. It is another way to align the school system's commitment to its focus.

Alignment of resources to adult learning was achieved in no small way by providing multiple options for attendance at professional learning sessions. Previously, when an athletic coach's duties conflicted with professional development, they may have been exempted from attending. It was possible to miss most of the formal professional growth opportunities offered throughout the year. Now, because everyone was accountable to become a teacher of literacy K-12, it was critical that all teachers attend literacy training sessions. Accordingly, teachers themselves suggested alternative times for professional development. For example, high school teachers designed sessions before school, after school, and at their planning times. Additional supports included the following:

- Staff could request to have strategies modeled in their classrooms.

- Data was made readily accessible so that teachers could hold data-based conversations with one another about their students.

- Literacy resources were purchased at teacher request.

A key alignment of resources to the system involved providing staff the opportunity to participate in decision making about their own professional learning. Given the data about their students' achievement, teachers grew increasingly competent about what they needed to know to meet students' needs. They were given the responsibility and resources to design much of their own professional learning. With its intentional alignment of resources the school system was able to "keep flying" at ever higher altitudes.

• **What non-monetary resources can we tap to improve the system?**

• **What networks can we develop to increase learning throughout the system?**

• **How can we ensure that everyone understands the direction of the system?**

Chapter 15

Capacity

Tough Questions:

- Who designs our learning?
- How do we invite many voices to participate?

Key Learning Principles:

- There is wisdom in the resistors.
- Adult learners know what they need to learn. Just ask them.
- People own only what they create. . .(Wheatley, 1992) or find meaningful.
- Design teams engage more voices and capture more intelligence in the system.
- Your work is my work; my work is your work.
- Participation needs to spread across all roles.

Main Ideas:

- School systems need expertise in using data to increase effectiveness in instruction.
- Participation allows us to create our own reality which we can then understand on our own terms.
- Formal leadership roles focus on the learning of students, staff, and individuals.
- Those in formal leadership positions use research-based practices that positively correlate with student achievement.

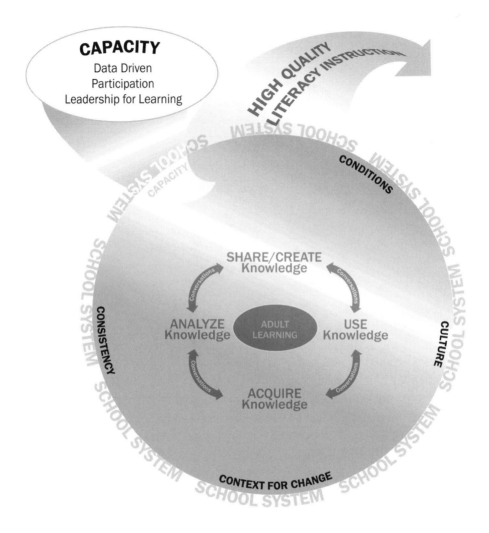

*D*efinition: Capacity is the potential to learn and grow the skills and knowledge that influences learning. In this story capacity is grown in the areas of data-driven decision making, participation, and leadership.

Capacity's Strategies:

- Data-Driven Decision Making
- Participation
- Leadership

Data-Driven Decision Making

How often have you scheduled a FLIGHT! without deciding upon your destination? How frequently do airlines neglect to monitor the number of passengers, the weight of the baggage, the amount of fuel, the mileage per flight? An airline's destinations and logistical information are all carefully documented and analyzed to maintain and improve productivity.

Likewise, school systems need expertise in using data in order to build their capacity and increase their effectiveness in instruction.

They need to be able to:

- manage data
- use data to set goals for authentic school improvement
- use data to guide instructional practice

MANAGE DATA

Northview took a rocky road to data management, initially. We naively believed that if the district purchased the best data warehouse system available, teachers would gather around their computers excitingly reviewing student data. This was a major misconception on the part of the district administration. Teachers could not use the original versions of the data warehouse because the warehouse produced very confusing graphics. This problem prompted administrators to reference their theory of change; they remembered the tenet, "There is wisdom in the resistors." As a result they honored varying perspectives and openly invited teacher feedback. "Tell us what you think, even if it's not what we want to hear."

Repeatedly, staff reported their concern over their inability to manage data. "The data warehouse should be easier to access and use. We need training at every staff meeting," was their cry. "How can one system meet the needs of all teachers, grades K-12? We need a common language about the warehouse so we can communicate with understanding. And by the way, how is this supposed to help us with instruction?"

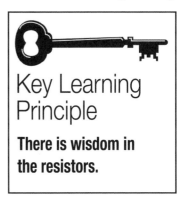

Key Learning Principle

There is wisdom in the resistors.

Although their responses were hard for administration to hear, teachers made clear that the warehouse was not meeting their needs. Prompted by staff's confusion and complaints, Stearns had the wisdom to ask a teacher for advice. Teacher Robin Paredez had a host of suggestions. Thus began a visioning process that would result in providing teachers with a valuable data management system.

Stearns and Grey engaged multiple staff members to design a data management system called FLIGHTS! which stands for "First Look Inquiry into Guiding, Helping, and Teaching Students." The developers' key question was, "What do you need to know?" Their product (a customized in-house website) pulls together the most requested student data into one central location. It is a record keeping system similar to that of a patient's medical history kept by a physician. The intent is for teachers to have quality, pertinent information at their fingertips to help unlock each student's potential "to fly."

Once teachers mastered the basics of FLIGHTS! they expressed a need for "real time" data to identify gaps in student learning for instructional planning. Staff commented, "With the new data warehouse we can find out anything about a student's progress and use it to help that student here and now."

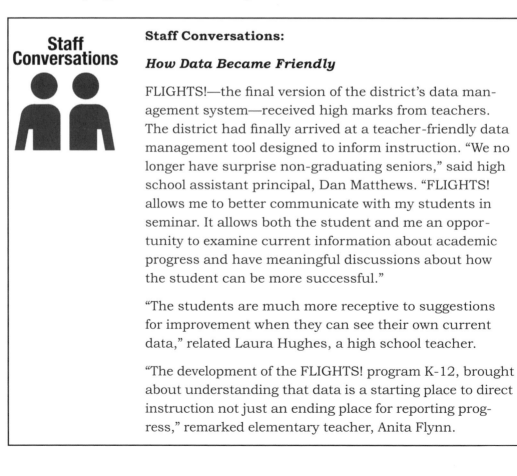

Staff Conversations

Staff Conversations:

How Data Became Friendly

FLIGHTS!—the final version of the district's data management system—received high marks from teachers. The district had finally arrived at a teacher-friendly data management tool designed to inform instruction. "We no longer have surprise non-graduating seniors," said high school assistant principal, Dan Matthews. "FLIGHTS! allows me to better communicate with my students in seminar. It allows both the student and me an opportunity to examine current information about academic progress and have meaningful discussions about how the student can be more successful."

"The students are much more receptive to suggestions for improvement when they can see their own current data," related Laura Hughes, a high school teacher.

"The development of the FLIGHTS! program K-12, brought about understanding that data is a starting place to direct instruction not just an ending place for reporting progress," remarked elementary teacher, Anita Flynn.

USE DATA

Northview had reached many milestones to monitor student learning. We had organized ourselves into learning communities, and acquired a data warehouse. We had developed the ability to store and retrieve data with ease. Now we needed to be able to analyze the data for implications for instruction. This requires a two-pronged skill set that enabled:

- learning together

- and translating the data into powerful information that can guide instructional planning.

An authentic school improvement process requires the use of data analysis skills. While adult learning is a social process, analyzing data is a technical process which is often missing from a district's repertoire of professional tools. Additionally, we needed to use data analysis skills from the perspective of the classroom, building, and district.

The more Northview learned about student data, the more we began to recognize possibilities to grow professional practice. Experience with assessment data makes clear the connections between assessment, curriculum, and instruction. The age-old assessment question of "How did they do?" gradually becomes "How did we do in teaching them?" a question of instruction; and "Are we assessing what we are teaching?" a question of curriculum and assessment.

These questions required staff to analyze demographic, outcome, and process data. Demographic data pinpoints the populations that are learning. Outcome data tells us what students have learned. Process data tells us the factors, such as curriculum that are influencing assessment results. From these three kinds of data, a school system can plan instructionally for

Key Learning Principle

Adult learners know what they need to learn. Just ask them.

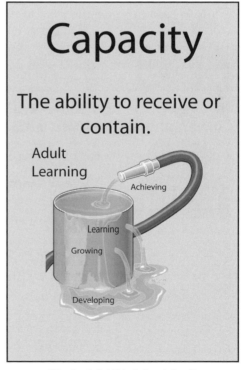

Capacity

The ability to receive or contain.

Student Art Work by John R.

students at the district, building, and classroom level (Wahlstrom, 1999). Equipped with this data, staff possesses the tools for a bona fide school improvement plan and for viewing all district students as a shared responsibility.

In a sense, school improvement is a type of "GPS" (global positioning system) which comes in handy in guiding our way. The school improvement process fosters the development of specific goals relative to achievement data. It serves as the roadmap to ensure that grade levels, buildings, and the district are moving in the same consistent direction. The process required that:

- staff analyze data to determine student needs.

- each grade level and building developed achievement goals specific for their unique population.

- buildings share their goals with one another.

- buildings look for common staff learning needs.

- goals are then knit together at the district level (Wahlstrom, 1999).

- teachers craft their own professional learning based on student need and school improvement goals.

The establishment of coordinated literacy goals at every level framed the district work in common vocabulary and practice.

Staff Conversations

A Conversation with Theresa Czarnopys, a District Assessment Consultant:

Helping Teachers Use Data for School Improvement

Theresa Czarnopys, serving as a district assessment consultant, says that in prior days a school improvement goal was selected "out of a hat." "The school's goal might be beautifying the parking lot, having kids line up better in the halls, or getting parents to do more at home with their kids. Often it had nothing to do with the data on student achievement."

Theresa worked with each building's school improvement team to help them determine a literacy goal based upon data. She challenged the teams to make sure

(continued)

teachers' instructional practice addressed the goal. Czarnopys relates, "Historically teachers were exposed to bits and pieces of school improvement, creating a fuzzy understanding at best. Given the use of data, teachers can see the 'big picture' of improving student achievement at the system, building, and classroom level. They intentionally make connections between the data and their own classroom practice. Classroom instruction now connects to the grade level and building goals. The district's tight school improvement process connects from classroom to classroom and school to school. It is a system-wide effort that connects us all to the vision and mission."

In the words of Judy Care, former Director of Instruction for Northview, "It used to be that the school improvement plan was done by the principal and sat in a notebook on a shelf collecting dust. No one thought it had any meaning; it was just another requirement from on high. Not any more. As part of this new school improvement process, teachers can pinpoint areas of student need from data. Then they have a role in designing the professional training they need. Each teacher at every grade level knows the goal because they helped determine it based upon the data they analyzed."

Staff Conversations

A Conversation with Cindi O'Connor, Elementary Principal:

School Improvement Provides a Clear Direction

Cindi O'Connor, a principal at North Oakview Elementary, cites two huge benefits of the upgraded school improvement process. "We set a goal in our building for writing, which was a low area on state assessments for our students. A representative team of teachers met and took an in depth look at our data. We narrowed our focus to specific skills that needed work at each grade level. Teachers drove the discussion to identify strategies to align with the goal. These strategies became the cornerstone of our work in literacy."

(continued)

> Cindi also credits her school improvement team with redesigning the building's master schedule to facilitate uninterrupted time for literacy. The data showed that literacy instruction was being delivered in choppy blocks of time. The team reworked the schedule for "specials" (time in art class, physical education, music, etc.) to provide more time for literacy instruction and grade level PLC meetings. The team revamped all available resources to provide additional intensive intervention.
>
> The North Oakview teachers held the belief that redesigning their schedule had to be grounded in what was best instructionally for students. Adult convenience was not a consideration. Kelly Rysberg, a fourth grade teacher in the building states, "The focus has shifted this year and the continuity has been great. Teachers' consistent use of the identified strategies has been helpful. The time we've invested in this planning has paid off. We have seen academic increases as a result of our school improvement changes."

This journey of using data, highlighted by the implementation of a data warehouse, was a major step in attaining a vision of high literacy achievement for all students.

Participation

Participation allows us to create our own reality which we then understand on our own terms. Only then are we willing to make a commitment. There are many reasons why participation is critical for building staff's capacity to learn:

- Participation builds ownership through recognizing value, meaning, and creating solutions.

- Participation is imperative to grow collective instructional practice.

- Participation creates energy to achieve the vision.

BUILD OWNERSHIP

According to Wheatley (1992) people need to have a say in how they will engage in their own work. They also need the opportunity to weigh in on the work of the district and their peers that is relevant to their own role.

"We know that the best way to build ownership is to give over the creation process to those who will be charged with its implementation. We are never successful if we merely present a plan in finished form to employees. It doesn't work to just ask people to sign on when they haven't been involved in the design process, when they haven't experienced the plan as a living, breathing thing . . . it is impossible to expect any plan or idea to be real to employees if they do not have the opportunity to personally interact with it. Reality emerges from our process of observation, from decisions we the observers make about what we will see. It does not exist independent of those activities. Therefore, we cannot talk people into reality because there truly is no reality to describe if they haven't been there. People can only become aware of the reality of the plan by interacting with it, by creating different possibilities throughout their personal processes of observation" (Wheatley, 1992, p. 67).

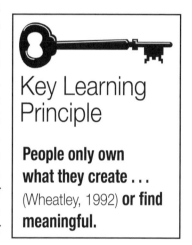

Key Learning Principle

People only own what they create . . . (Wheatley, 1992) **or find meaningful.**

One of our foundation's representatives related that he often prepared data presentations for the foundation's board of directors. He would take his presentations to his teammates so that they could learn from the data themselves and give him feedback for possible upgrades. Every time he took a draft presentation to this group, no matter the quality, his teammates sliced and dissected it. They offered numerous suggestions. He would take good notes, ask engaging questions, and encourage his teammates' critiques. Eventually, having worked hard to understand it, the team would approve his presentation.

The foundation representative would genuinely thank his team for their input. He knew that the intent of their comments was not criticism. Instead, his teammates needed to connect the information to their own knowledge in order to make this presentation meaningful to themselves. Only then could they commit to it.

Historically in Northview central office staff designed learning opportunities for teachers, assuming that they knew what teachers needed. Thus it was possible for central office to miss the mark because they often did not invite teachers to design their own learning opportunities based on data.

According to Wheatley (1992, p. 64), a few people have the ability to observe "only a very few of the potentialities contained within that data. However, we found that when multiple people are involved in looking at the data and the information is spread out broadly, many interpretations appear." When staff was engaged in discussions about their data and their needs, new combinations and conclusions were generated. Our understanding of our practice was enhanced by participating with many others who share varying and sometimes novel perspectives.

Key Learning Principle

Design teams engage more voices and capture more intelligence in the system.

Northview now relies on staff to identify instructional needs and creatively plan how to meet them. We recognized the need for many voices and interpretations of the available data. When staff participates, central office no longer has to shoulder the responsibility for all the answers. Sharing ownership for the learning enhances the quality of the work. Solutions are more creative improving instructional practice system wide.

To foster staff's ownership and participation, Brayman, our critical friend, introduced the concept of design teams. The intent of design teams is to have staff actually in the pilot's seat, planning their own learning. Anyone from any level in the system can volunteer to be on a design team. Teams build individual and school system capacity by including a variety of participants each time. Participation is not only encouraged, but expected.

Staff Conversations

A Conversation With Maureen Grey, Director of Instruction:

Design Teams Are Our Way of Doing Business

Maureen Grey, then Director of Instruction stated, "Design Teams have become our method to plan our work and make sure we are including everyone in the process. There is great benefit in this. It fosters support and understanding for initiatives throughout the entire district. Everyone's contributions are celebrated. Invariably our original ideas are modified and made better because we used the design team process."

Design teams convene for each adult learning opportunity as well as building and district meetings. Before the staff members actually meet, the design team networks with the staff and solicits their ideas for consideration. A design team's planning template may include:

- participants who will be affected by the outcome
- identified outcomes for the meeting
- pertinent information, quantitative or qualitative
- a draft of the agenda
- specific times for each agenda item
- persons responsible and responsibilities
- detailed logistics
- resources needed
- a communication plan.

Some grumble that a design team process may take longer, but the end results are worthwhile. According to staff members it is time well spent and honors the participants' needs. Jenny Barnes, an elementary teacher comments, "I feel like, as a district, with design teams we are working more efficiently and effectively to make better use of our time, guiding staff toward better learning."

GROWING COLLECTIVE INSTRUCTIONAL PRACTICE

Across the system, Northview's staff expressed the desire to use data more effectively to guide instructional practice. Volunteer staff, calling themselves the Data Diggers, provided the solution. They initially were the "go to" people in the buildings for technology challenges. The Data Digger's group invited any interested staff into their ranks. These Data Digger "super hubs" were teachers' guides. Their easy access made data-learning and data use "just-in-time, job embedded, and on-going."

The Data Diggers provided an invaluable service to staff. They put data in teachers' hands so that teachers could analyze it collaboratively while engaging in substantive conversations. Later, the Data Diggers helped teachers track and interpret their data. With this support teachers were enabled to make adjustments in their instructional planning. They grew the capacity of the entire staff to use data for improving their professional practice.

CREATE ENERGY TO ACHIEVE THE VISION

Wheatley (1992) suggests that when people participate with one another, sharing their information, creativity abounds, and innovation increases.

Staff Conversations

A Conversation with Kathy Vogel, Seventh Grade Teacher:

Creating Energy for the District's Vision

Kathy Vogel, a seventh grade teacher and co-chair of the district's language arts committee, created energy for Northview by inviting staff members to learn and grow in literacy. She offered book clubs, strategy demonstrations, and end-of-summer, "Cool Ideas for Back to School" workshop sessions. She was instrumental in designing the district's literacy coaching network. While the district adopted a K-12 literacy focus and framework, Vogel worked the sidelines to build broad participation. She said, "I want my colleagues to contribute to the framework and have the skills to teach the literacy strategies so students benefit."

What's special about Kathy Vogel? The answer is nothing and yet everything. She created a spark that ignited staff's enthusiasm for the system focus. She thinks beyond the walls of her classroom to facilitate system-wide participation in literacy learning. Staff creates energy when they share practices with each other. Vogel is a catalyst for that energy through staff learning efforts. Ultimately these efforts impact student achievement.

Staff Conversations

A Conversation with Kathy Skudre, Paraprofessional:

Creating Energy by Supporting the District's Vision

Kathy Skudre serves an important role in her school. As the library/media paraprofessional, she had her ear to the ground. She had a long tenure with the district and felt a responsibility to assist teachers in meeting their goals.

According to Dan Duba, Highlands' principal, "Thanks to an inclusive climate of collaboration, we are welcoming everyone's participation. Kathy jumped on board by attending literacy meetings in the hopes of helping teachers and students."

Skudre shares, "Teachers were designing learning stations to promote collaborative learning opportunities in their classrooms. I can share my expertise with them and get them up and running. It energizes me to know that I am making a difference."

A system can build capacity by valuing everyone's contribution. "Knowledge is generated anew from connections that weren't there before" (Wheatley, 1992, p.115). "Through constant exchanges, new information is spawned, and the organization grows in effectiveness" (p. 116).

Leadership for Learning

If you could choose a pilot for your FLIGHT! what criteria would you use for your selection? Gender? Intelligence? Amount of training? Extent of experience? Interpersonal skills? Track record for safe FLIGHTS!? Most of us would choose the latter. We want someone who can get us where we are going safely. So how would we describe formal school leaders "who can get us there?" And what is "there?"

Effective leaders know that no single person is capable of getting us "there" but they know how to move an organization forward by motivating staff with the power of shared leadership. "Successful implementation of organizational change . . .

requires strong leadership on the part of positional leaders such as superintendents, central office administrators, and principals" (Conzemius and O'Neill, 2001).

For example Superintendent Stearns and Director of Instruction Grey knew that in order for teachers to collaborate they needed professional development. They provided training in a professional learning community's model which fostered the development of teacher leaders. In order for teachers to "step up," the leadership

Student Art Work by Brooklyn V.

in the central office had to create the opportunities for growth and an environment which allowed shared leadership to flourish.

Although there are countless descriptors of desirable school leaders, and we each have our own preference for how we want to be led, the bottom line remains: school leaders are ultimately responsible for leading the schooling effort to high levels of achievement for each and every student. When all of our students are achieving at high levels, we "have arrived—there." How do we find leaders who are capable of this tall order? Are they born into leadership capacity? Perhaps they take classes and learn leadership skills. Maybe they are promoted from the classroom and are expected to figure it out, a little baptism by fire.

Effective leadership reflects the complexity of the schooling effort. The role of leaders is to focus on the learning and achievement of students as well as the learning of staff and the leaders themselves. This renders them "Leaders for Learning."

The school system expects that leaders exercise rigorous discipline in the use of best educational leadership practices. Formal leaders are accountable for student achievement. They need to ensure that students are learning. Leaders for learning require a research base for their chosen leadership practices. Additionally development of leadership-for-learning capability demands a sophisticated understanding of pedagogy (student learning), androgogy (adult learning), and systems thinking.

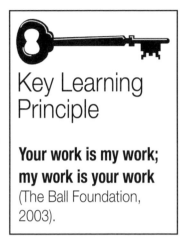

Key Learning Principle

Your work is my work; my work is your work
(The Ball Foundation, 2003).

Like every other practice in this book, the leadership-for-learning capacity can be developed. Its depth and breadth are limited only by knowledge, energy, and time. The sustainability of leadership-for-learning is dependent upon implementation of an identified set of best practices and commitment to continuous learning.

Learning leaders continually ask, "What is working?" Much to the benefit of all those in formal learning leadership roles, McREL (Midcontinent Regional Educational Laboratory, 2005) has completed extensive research on the relationship of school and district leadership and student achievement. Their findings suggest that when district and school leaders engage in effective leadership behavior, student achievement is positively affected.

Richard Elmore reported in a study for the National Governors' Association, "Knowing the right thing to do is the central problem of school improvement. Holding schools accountable for their performance depends on having people in schools with the knowledge, skill, and judgment to make the improvements that will increase student performance" (p. 9).

BUILDING-LEVEL LEADERSHIP FOR LEARNING

So what is the "right thing" for learning leaders to do? For building-level leaders, McREL (Midcontinent Regional Educational Laboratory, 2005) research identified twenty-one leadership practices that positively correlate with student achievement when the leader is focused on instructional improvement. This research also pinpoints seven practices that correlate highly with student achievement. The table below outlines the responsibilities and the associated practices for leaders and connects them to Northview's authentic work.

Using Best Practices in Leadership

RESPONSIBILITY (Marzano, Waters, McNulty, 2005, pp. 15-16)	ASSOCIATED PRACTICES (Marzano, Waters, McNulty, 2005, pp. 15-16)	BEST PRACTICES APPLIED in Northview's Authentic Work
Knowledge of curriculum, instruction, assessment	• Is knowledgeable about the curriculum and instructional practices • Is knowledgeable about assessment practices • Provides conceptual guidance for teachers regarding effective classroom practice	• Facilitated curriculum alignment and development of common assessments • Shifted meeting agendas to conversations about instruction • Pursued formal training on effective assessment practices • Used instructional and literacy framework as standards for effective classroom practice • Used data for decisions on curriculum, instruction, and assessment
Optimizer	• Inspires teachers and staff to accomplish things that might seem beyond their grasp • Portrays a positive attitude about the ability of teachers and staff to accomplish substantial things • Is a driving force behind major initiatives	• Framed conversations from an "asset-based" perspective • Built on staff strengths • Facilitated instructional improvement • Aligned resources and use of best practices to the district focus
Intellectual Stimulation	• Stays informed about current research and theory regarding effective schooling • Continually exposes teachers and staff to cutting-edge ideas about how to be effective • Systematically engages teachers and staff in discussions about current research and theory • Continually involves teachers and staff in reading articles and books about effective practices	• Engaged in book studies with peers at administrative retreats • Facilitated teacher access to outside and inside experts for modeling and dialogue • Engaged staff in conversations about best practices • Aligned resources of time and materials for teachers to study effective practices

RESPONSIBILITY (Marzano, Waters, McNulty, 2005, pp. 15-16)	**ASSOCIATED PRACTICES** (Marzano, Waters, McNulty, 2005, pp. 15-16)	**BEST PRACTICES APPLIED** in Northview's Authentic Work
Change agent	• Consciously challenges the status quo • Is comfortable leading change initiatives with uncertain outcomes • Systematically considers new and better ways of doing things	• Asked tough questions about teachers', peers' and one's own practice • Challenged and encouraged staff to innovate • Used the principles of the change process to guide implementation of initiatives • Participated in administrators' PLC team
Monitors/evaluates	• Monitors and evaluates the effectiveness of the curriculum • Monitors and evaluates the effectiveness of instruction • Monitors and evaluates the effectiveness of assessment	• Systematically engaged staff in the use of data to focus on evidence of learning • Rigorously supported staff in developing their own learning • Continually implemented a school improvement process that targeted students' learning needs and staff's instructional needs • Encouraged and provided coaching to staff on best practices
Flexibility	• Is comfortable with major changes in how things are done • Encourages people to express opinions that may be contrary to those held by individuals in positions of authority • Adapts leadership style to needs of specific situations • Can be directive or non-directive as the situation warrants	• Viewed change as a constant factor in the work • Sought and valued diverse opinions • Created an open culture for shared leadership and participation
Ideals/Beliefs	• Holds strong professional ideals and beliefs about schooling, teaching, and learning • Shares ideals and beliefs about schooling, teaching, and learning with teachers, staff, and parents • Demonstrates behaviors that are consistent with ideals and beliefs	• Shared values and beliefs about education with stakeholders • Aligned behavior with espoused values and beliefs to promote consistency, trust, and quality relationships • Modeled that continual learning is required to improve instructional practice • Viewed family and community involvement as an important factor of student achievement

The following are detailed examples of three of Marzano, Waters, and McNulty's research-based practices (2005) in Northview's authentic work:

- knowledge of instruction

- change agent

- intellectual stimulation

Key Learning Principle

Participation needs to spread across all roles.

Knowledge of High Quality Instruction

Learning-leaders need to understand what kinds of instruction help students use their minds well. Research indicates that students are most successful when they engage in active, relevant learning and use new knowledge in real-world application. Newmann and Wehlage, contributors to curriculum development at state levels, suggest that educators use a set of standards to design optimal instruction. The chart "Five Standards for Authentic Instruction" (1993), shown on the following page, explains critical components of quality instruction that provoke significant and meaningful learning.

From a set of learning standards or principles, we adopted a basic framework for instruction. The advantage of an instructional framework is three-fold:

1. It helps us align how we teach with how students learn.

2. It provides a standard for quality instruction throughout the entire system.

3. It eliminates the inefficiencies of various instructional approaches as students transition from teacher to teacher, from grade to grade.

With a common instructional framework, Northview principals conversed knowledgeably with all staff about instruction. They used the same language. The instructional framework took the guess work out of, "How is this lesson being delivered so that students learn?" This in itself promoted accountability between the administrators and their staff.

With an instructional framework, leaders are able to define quality instruction. This promotes objectivity in observation. No longer do leaders have to rely on their own past experience or training to conjure up a personal definition of quality instruction. The standard has already been established. For staff, the instructional framework clarifies what quality teaching is.

Five Standards for Authentic Instruction

STANDARD	SUPPORTING INFORMATION
Higher Order Thinking	"Higher order thinking requires students to manipulate information and ideas in ways that transform their meaning and implications, such as when students combine facts and ideas in order to synthesize, generalize, explain, hypothesize, or arrive at some conclusion or interpretation. Manipulating information and ideas through these processes allows students to solve problems and discover new (for them) meanings and understandings."
Depth of Knowledge	"Knowledge is deep or thick when it concerns the central ideas of a topic or discipline. For students, knowledge is deep when they make clear distinctions, develop arguments, solve problems, construct explanations, and otherwise work with relatively complex understandings. Depth is produced, in part, by covering fewer topics in systematic and connected ways."
Connectedness to the World	"A lesson gains in authenticity the more there is a connection to the larger social context within which students live. Instruction can exhibit some degree of connectedness when (1) students address real-world public problems. . .; or (2) students use personal experiences as a context for applying knowledge (such as using conflict resolution techniques in their own school)."
Substantive Conversation	"High levels of substantive conversation are indicated by three features: 1. There is considerable interaction about the ideas of a topic (the talk is about disciplined subject matter and includes indicators of higher-order thinking such as making distinctions, applying ideas, forming generalizations, raising questions, and not just reporting experiences, facts, definitions, or procedures. 2. Sharing of ideas is evident in exchanges that are not completely scripted or controlled. . . . 3. The dialogue builds coherently on participants' ideas to promote improved collective understanding of a theme or topic."

continued next page

Five Standards for Authentic Instruction—continued

Social Support for Student Achievement	"Social support is high in classes when the teacher conveys high expectations for all students, including that it is necessary to take risks and try hard to master challenging academic work, that all members of the class can learn important knowledge and skills, and that a climate of mutual respect among all members of the class contributes to achievement by all. "Mutual respect" means that all students with less skill or proficiency in a subject are treated in ways that encourage their efforts and value their contributions."

(pp. 2-5)

Change Agent

How excited would we be to fly with a pilot who did not use his vast training when operating an aircraft? "Let me off this plane!" would most likely be our cry. Similarly, learning-leaders are responsible to use their knowledge of the change process because of the broad implications change has for their school system. Northview used the tenets of change explained previously in Chapter 12:

- Change should be based on a shared vision and communicated clearly to all.

- Change is experienced as a loss by many.

- There is often wisdom in resistance.

- Change should permeate the organization.

- Change is both individual and organizational.

- Evaluation is an important part of the change process.

Learning-leaders demonstrate knowledge of the importance of change to the school system. They display the courage to endure the challenges of change yet are sensitive to staff's needs.

When stakeholders resist change, it is imperative that learning-leaders communicate explicitly the advantages of the change (Bennis and Nanus, 1985). Stakeholders need to fully understand the correlation between change and the vision of the school system.

Formal learning-leaders need to realize that although that connection may be readily evident to them, it may be lost on others who do not deal day to day with big picture issues. Learning-leaders' mantra of change needs to be, "This is what we know. Based on our data, this is where we are going. This is why. This is how the change will foster the attainment of our vision." It is sometimes necessary to spell out the risks inherent in not proceeding with change. Learning-leaders caution, "If we do not make these important changes, we are going to have increased challenges down the road."

Then with great courage learning-leaders ask, "And what might you know to validate or repudiate this change?" With open minds they seek dissonant information to which they may not be privy. They consider this information carefully without consideration of their own ego needs, making adjustments as indicated. Finally learning-leaders inquire and gather information from stakeholders as to how change can best be implemented. "What do we know has worked before? What assets might we build upon? What is doable? Who has the most knowledge among us to help lead the charge?"

Robert Evans (1996) explains that supportive administrative leadership is crucial to effective change. "Considerable experience confirms that [the ability to] progress from loss to commitment benefits enormously from personal contact between the leaders and the targets of change" (p. 62). He relates, "A key way that teachers' needs for continuity can be sustained is by regular contact with a sympathetic principal who will acknowledge the distress they are experiencing even as she reconfirms the promise of change and reinforces the necessity and promise of the new skills required" (p. 63).

Northview's leaders extended staff the respect and time needed to work through changes. Communications did not demand or threaten. Instead leaders respectfully shared and elicited information, then repeatedly engaged stakeholders. With ongoing guidance from administrators, teachers had the supports to develop their competence with the shared understanding of the change process. Initially it was a process of leading for learning, then learning for leading.

Intellectual Stimulation: Administrators' PLC's

If you were a pilot and knew of a route that consistently provided a swift FLIGHT!, chances are you would opt to use that route on a regular basis. So too, did the principals of Northview elect to create a professional learning community (PLC) to accelerate their learning. This structure provided a forum wherein they could efficiently develop their capacity as learning-leaders.

Although most administrative meeting agendas are stuffed with administrivia, Stearns and Grey worked to focus the Northview administrative agenda on instruction. They encouraged the administrative team to design an agenda around leadership for learning. Time was set aside in each meeting for the team to engage in professional conversations about current issues, mostly instructional. Just like their respective staffs, they gathered their data; they analyzed it, shared and created new knowledge, and tried out resultant solutions. Then they would begin again at the next meeting by sharing their data: What worked? What did not? Why? What has worked for you? Is there a different, more effective way of employing this practice?

Richard DuFour and Robert Marzano (2009, p. 63) suggest, "When principals make the transition from instructional leaders to learning leaders, they move the conversation from "What was taught?" or "How was it taught?" to the far more important questions of "What was learned?" and "How can we use evidence of learning to strengthen our professional practice?"

To hone their professional skills, the administrative team became collaborators in learning. The PLC venue lent itself to sharing what was important to each administrator at that moment in time. The learning cycle facilitated sharing and creating "just-in-time solutions" for pressing as well as long-term problems. The administrative team grew to rely on the knowledge and wisdom of their peers and became increasingly accountable to one another for implementing their new learning. Additionally they saw themselves as a collaborative team, growing and supporting each other.

DISTRICT-LEVEL LEADERSHIP FOR LEARNING

Waters and Marzano (2006) conducted parallel research to determine the influence of superintendents on student achievement. Their analyses reveal that, indeed, district-level leadership matters. What did they find were effective practices for superintendents? The chart on the following page explains their findings about the superintendent's specific responsibilities and describes what they looked like in authentic work in Northview.

Richard DuFour and Robert Marzano (2009) suggest a new interpretation of the role of formal leadership. "We advocate for a new image. If the fundamental purpose of schools is to ensure that all students learn at high levels, then schools do not need instructional leaders—they need learning-leaders who focus on evidence of learning" (p. 63).

DuFour and Marzano (2009) challenge school systems to redefine administrative priorities. All leaders-for-learning are responsible to do "what works." This mandates a commitment to use best practices in an intentional way. Should those efforts fail to produce required results, leaders need to be innovative in finding new ways of working.

EFFECTIVE SUPERINTENDENT PRACTICES (Waters, Marzano, 2006, pp. 3-4)	APPLICATION IN NORTHVIEW'S AUTHENTIC WORK
1. Collaborative goal-setting	• Stearns and Grey engaged stakeholders in the revision of the district vision, mission, strategic plan, and literacy focus. • They enlisted the district literacy committee to draft the literacy framework and communicate its importance.
2. Setting goals that all staff members must act upon in student achievement and classroom instruction	• Stearns, Grey, the administrative team, and staff revised the school improvement process. • They used data to set high, yet attainable, student achievement goals. • They collectively determined best practice instructional strategies to achieve them.
3. Board alignment and support of district goals	• Stearns and Grey communicated the literacy focus to the Board of Education which in turn aligned its goals and policies. • The entire district shared one set of unified goals.
4. Monitoring goals for achievement and instruction	• Stearns, Grey, along with the district school improvement team, monitored student progress from a district perspective. • The principals and building staffs monitored student achievement at the building and classroom levels.
5. Use of resources to support achievement and instructional goals	• Stearns, Grey, and the administrative team obtained staff recommendations and aligned district resources with the literacy focus.

- *What is the power of inviting learners to design their own learning?*

- *What is the value of listening to skeptics, worriers, and critics?*

- *How do we make sure that best practices constitute the bulk of our day-to-day work?*

Chapter 16

Consistency

Tough Question:

- How can we build consistent practice and increase student achievement simultaneously?

Carry-On

Key Learning Principle:

- Efficiency and effectiveness are the result of knowing where we are going and what we are doing.

Main Ideas:

- The vision binds staff together in an unwavering, common purpose; it is the basis upon which decisions are made.

- Using an instructional framework and school-wide literacy practices increases consistency of practice and the efficiency of student learning.

- The predictability of an unwavering vision and professional practice builds integrity and trust.

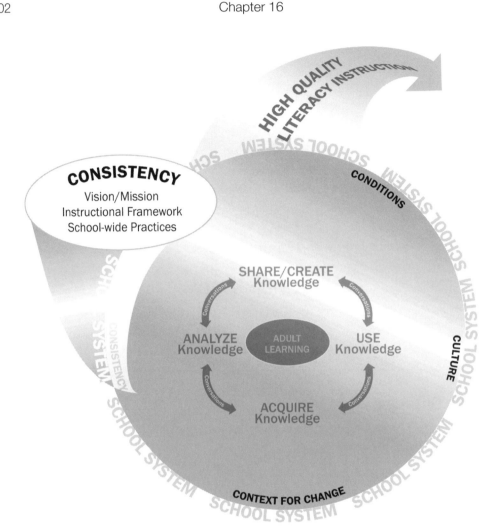

*D*efinition: Consistency is the predictability of behavior and practice which builds trust (Vaill, 1989). When the vision and mission guide all decision making, staff can trust that they share the same purpose and are heading in the same direction (Bennis and Nanus, 1985). Additionally, the use of consistent instructional practices across the K-12 system increases student achievement.

On one occasion former Director of Instruction Grey had the opportunity to drive a nationally renowned literacy expert to the airport, after a presentation to Northview and Kent County teachers. Seizing the opportunity to corner this expert, Grey posed questions that she had been pondering. "So, of all the excellent research-based strategies, which one is the best? Which one makes the biggest difference in student achievement? What gives schools the biggest bang for the educational buck?"

Without hesitation, the expert confided, "There's no one best strategy. *It almost doesn't matter what a school chooses* as its school-wide literacy practices or strategies. The *biggest thing is that they are consistent.* Staff needs to come to agreements, and all do whatever they agree to do. It's the consistency that's the magic ingredient. It's not rocket science. It's really pretty simple."

Consistency's Strategies:

- Commitment to Vision and Mission

- Instructional Framework

- Shared Practices

Commitment to Vision and Mission

The school system's vision is the most fundamental statement of its values, beliefs, and goals. It communicates where the school system is today and creates the best and brightest picture of what the system wants to be. This vision is the unwavering standard for all decision making. It provides the compass for all the system's FLIGHTS! Staff can identify with a powerful vision statement. It binds them together in a common, higher purpose.

Judy Care, former Director of Instruction, often remarked, "People do not leave Northview. Once hired, they stay." There are no extraordinary benefits in Northview's contract to entice employees to put down such strong roots. Instead, staff shares a sense of belonging to something more important than themselves.

That commitment to something bigger than ourselves draws us to our work like a moth to the light. The school system's vision is a catalyst for building a strong individual and collective identity that establishes who we are in the world and what we are becoming. "Visions are always about a future state; a condition that does not presently exist and never existed before" (Bennis and Nanus, 1985, pp. 89-90). This shared picture becomes the "North Star" for what the district should attend to.

"When the organization has a clear sense of its purpose, direction, and desired future state and when this image is widely shared, individuals are able to find their own roles both in the organization and in the larger society. . . . This empowers individuals and confers status upon them because they can see themselves as part of a worthwhile enterprise. They gain a sense of importance, as they are transformed . . . to human beings engaged in a creative and purposeful venture" (Bennis and Nanus, 1985, pp. 90-91).

A key responsibility of leaders is engaging their people in building a common sense of purpose to insure stability and consistency. Each stakeholder brings their own individual purpose to the school setting. The challenge of leadership is to weave all of those unique visions into a collective one that inspires everyone's work to the same end. Senge (1990) emphasizes the power of a shared vision. "When more people come to share a common vision, the vision may not change fundamentally. But it comes more alive, more real in the sense of a mental reality that people can truly imagine achieving. They now have partners, 'co-creators'; the vision no longer rests on their shoulders alone" (p. 212).

Staff Conversations

A Conversation with Janice Crawford, the Senior Fellow at The Ball Foundation

Janice repeatedly admonished her foundation colleagues, "We *must* base all of our decisions on our vision/mission. It is the reason we are all here. We cannot waver from this purpose or we risk losing our way. In my former employment our team used to have decidedly different perspectives which led to many conflicts in problem solving. Our discussions were often tense and heated. But we knew that we were all charged to align our final outcome with the district's vision/mission. No matter the level of consternation or the final outcome, our relationships remained solid because we were bound together as a team by our commitment to this consistent direction."

THE RELATIONSHIP OF THE VISION AND THE MISSION TO CHANGE

Senge (1990) notes the importance of planning for change by building a common vision. Leaders must have a vision that is shared by everyone in the system. True commitment depends on a common picture of the future that people are trying to create.

The Northview staff developed a powerful mission statement that connected instructional practice with student learning. Ask teachers in any school district what their mission statement is, and they may not be able to recite it. In Northview they can. This is because the Northview mission statement was developed by staff. It reflects their work and resonates across the K-12 spectrum.

Throughout the district administrators posed the question of teachers, "What is your work?" Regardless of content area or grade level, staff concurred that they had to prepare students for their next set of learnings, responsibilities, and challenges. This theme of preparation was embodied in the Northview mission statement:

"PREPARING STUDENTS FOR LIFE'S NEXT STEP!"

The mission statement soon became the cornerstone in Northview's culture, as reflected in the testimonies of students. The following letter, titled "My Expectations," was written by a Northview High School student to explain his understanding of the meaning of the mission statement.

My Expectations

"Preparing students for life's next step." When I first read this mission statement, it sounded like fortune cookie lingo, like the kind of statement you would hear at an educational convention. However, over the past three years, this phrase has become more than the mission statement of my school. I truly believe it is the promise that every teacher, every secretary, and every member of this administration have made to the students they serve.

I first asked myself, "What is life's next step?" Is it college—maybe a university, or is it getting a job, or raising a family. Is life's next step simply spending the next thirty years preparing for retirement? Maybe, maybe not. The people I have met at Northview have led me to believe that life's next step is following a dream, to challenge myself and to reach out and touch the world. For one person it may be going to college; for someone else it may be expressing themselves to the world through the arts. Life's next step cannot be defined; it is whatever you wish it to be—whatever you dream.

Northview High School is dedicated to the development of students. The staff commits its time to not only teaching about reading, writing, and arithmetic, but about life. They guide their students in matters of morality, respect, cooperation, teamwork, setting goals, and perseverance. More important than academics, they believe that "Preparing students for life's next step" means instructing students on how to use their talents and abilities to create something the world desires.

Nationally, fifteen percent of high school students do not graduate. In the past four years Northview High School has only had one student not graduate. Moreover, 80-86% of Northview graduates attend a two-year or four-year college program after graduation. That is why Northview is a National Blue Ribbon School. Northview Public Schools prepare students for life's next step.

How does Northview prepare me for life's next step? Since the first day I came to this school, I have been provided with the best teachers. I have never met a teacher here who I have not been able to associate with on a personal level. Many teachers have become more than mere instructors for me; they have become my counselors, role models, and most importantly-my friends. This comfort level that has arisen between my teachers and me has led them to sharing stories about their lives, their mistakes, and their successes through which I have learned more than I ever could have with a traditional education.

The teachers at Northview wholeheartedly care, not only about my academic success, but also about my personal goals. Whenever I read Northview's mission statement, I think about people here that have influenced me and have helped me succeed in doing everything I can to prepare for my life's next step.

I walk through the doors of this school everyday with expectations that many other schools' students can't imagine. I enter a world where I will be challenged, strengthened, and nourished with the knowledge that staff allows me to take hold of my dream and soar above the waters of success. Northview's mission statement is so much more than a motto; it is a way of life that sets this school system apart from the rest. I believe it is a promise to every student who comes through this school system and is a goal that every staff member here strives for.

In schools shared vision generates energy and commitment to one's role, to one another, and to the system. It provides a lofty target which challenges staff to learn about their instructional practice. According to Senge (1990, p. 209), "Shared vision fosters risk taking and experimentation." For Northview, it brought consistency to its focus and practice.

Instructional Framework

Northview had developed a literacy framework comprised of research-based literacy strategies. However, staff recognized a big omission. The framework lacked a consistent method to deliver instruction in K-12 classrooms. Back at the drawing board, the literacy committee chose the Gradual Release of Responsibility Model (Pearson and Fielding, 1991). In the *Language Arts Workshop* book, the authors, Nancy Frey and Doug Fisher (2006, p. 5), explain, "The Gradual Release of Responsibility Model is a widely used model of instruction that begins with explicit instruction of a skill or strategy then moves to guided instruction as students try it on for themselves. . . ."

The Gradual Release of Responsibility model is simply that. The teacher primarily shoulders the responsibility for the learning in the early phase, and then eventually turns over the responsibility for using the strategy or skill to the learners as they become more competent and prepared.

Frey and Fisher suggest, "As powerful as this model of instruction is, it will not be successful without connections to the lives of learners. Meaningful experiences enhance learning acquisition because the student can apply the new knowledge to the situation. A basic premise of learning is that when experiences are meaningful to the learner, the ability to learn increases" (pp. 5-6).

The sequence of instruction can be described as an "I do it, we do it, you do it," pattern (Frey and Fisher, 2006, p. 6). In the first phase, the teacher demonstrates how something is done ("I do it"). Next, the student attempts the task with the teacher leading them through the process ("We do it"). Then the student tries it with a partner ("You do it"). Ultimately the expectation is that the student is able to use the strategy independently ("You do it alone").

When teachers in content areas use the Gradual Release of Responsibility model they:

- model for and support students. The teacher serves as the expert demonstrating the information, skill, or strategy and how to use it.

- provide layers of instruction to guide the learning. They scaffold instruction, build a base for comprehension, and check for understanding.

- provide opportunities for meaningful activities with peers and partners while applying the information and deepening understanding.

- design assignments so that students can individually practice and apply what they have learned.

Frey and Fisher's graphic (2006, p. 6) depicts the shifting of responsibility from teacher instruction to student learning. This model can be applied in any teaching/learning sequence.

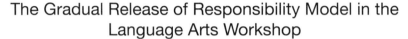

The Gradual Release of Responsibility Model in the Language Arts Workshop

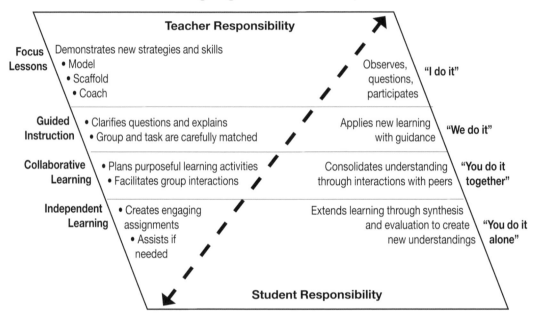

Frey & Fisher, LANGUAGE ARTS WORKSHOP, Figure 1.1, p. 6, copyright 2006 by Pearson Education, Inc. Reproduced by permission of Pearson Education, Inc.

Northview teachers observed demonstration lessons of the gradual release model in a variety of subjects across grade levels. Literacy coaches modeled each component of the instructional design. Following the lesson, a debrief time allowed teachers to reflect on and inquire about the lesson. The teachers then dialogued with peers about how the lesson related to their own instruction.

Using the Gradual Release of Responsibility model grew the teacher's capacity to consistently support student learning. This instructional framework increased students' understanding and ownership of their learning. Northview adopted this instructional framework, K-12, to support consistency of practice, increased learning, and more effective instruction.

Shared Literacy Practices

It is becoming increasingly understood that a school can impact student achievement when it employs a school wide focus on literacy instruction. Rebecca Jones (2006) suggests, "A district gets the biggest bang for its literacy buck by simply redirecting its professional development money to help teachers use literacy-based strategies across the curriculum. 'If students are being taught literacy skills across the curriculum in every class, your average students' reading scores will improve,' says Susan Frost" (p. 34). Frost was advisor to Richard Riley, former U.S. Secretary of Education.

Key Learning Principle

Efficiency and effectiveness are the result of knowing where we are going and what we are doing.

Literacy strategies are articulated in a literacy framework. This tool brings consistency to common literacy practices. Doug Fisher and Nancy Frey (2004, p. 3) ask and then relate, "How do we know that literacy instruction in all content areas matters? The evidence is mounting." A study by Fisher (2001) suggested that a school wide focus on literacy instruction could impact student achievement.

They continue (p. 3), "Further evidence can be found in Reeves' (2000) study of highly effective schools. Schools described as 90/90/90 (90% free/reduced lunch, 90% ethnic minorities, and 90% at or above mastery level on standardized achievement tests) were analyzed for common factors. These characteristics included a school wide focus on achievement, agreed upon curriculum choices, and an emphasis on writing (Reeves, 2000). It is possible that many schools who have not achieved the same levels of success as the 90/90/90 schools share these same characteristics. However, we believe that the key to success lies in another part of the report. All of these high achievement schools shared another important element—they stick with their plans. These schools, 'are not lurching from one fad to another . . . they are consistent'" (p. 193).

Northview designed professional learning around school wide literacy practices. A school wide literacy practice, determined by student achievement data, is intended to be consistently used by teachers within a building and between buildings. The practices, or strategies, are research-based and can be applied in various content areas with flexibility.

Staff Conversations	**A Conversation with Robin Paredez, Northview High School Teacher:**

Staff Conversations

A Conversation with Robin Paredez, Northview High School Teacher:

Students Benefit From Consistent Practices

Robin Paredez, a high school Spanish and mathematics teacher says, "I see the awesome results of having shared common vocabulary for students as they move from grade to grade. We need to remember that students move from teacher to teacher throughout the day and over the years. As teachers the least we can do is to have common practices and common vocabulary so students don't have to relearn those. Then they can focus upon the content."

There are many examples of school wide strategies from which to choose. Use of concept maps, a type of graphic organizer, is one such strategy designed to more actively engage students with reading.

"Graphic organizers are visual displays of information, often arranged in bubbles or squares with connecting lines between them that are used to portray conceptual relationships" (Fisher, Brozo, Frey, Ivey, 2007, p. 10). One benefit of using concept maps is that students must reread text. This forces them to think about what they are reading and then create a visual demonstrating their understanding.

Bromley, Irwin-DeVitis, and Modlo (1995) are proponents of K-12 consistency through the use of graphic organizers. "Traditionally, graphic organizers have been used by content area teachers to represent organization. Typically, graphic organizers are used to show the structure of information in materials from a science or social studies book. But virtually all sources of knowledge—not just print—contain meaning that can be represented in graphic organizers. For example, information and ideas presented through film, lecture, video, and discussion can be organized and depicted graphically. As elementary and secondary school teachers use graphic organizers to help their students learn concepts and information, we encourage them to widen the arena of graphic organizer's use" (pp. 8-9).

The appeal in Northview of selecting concept maps and graphic organizers as a school wide strategy was that they were readily understood by various content teachers at all levels. Many had already successfully used these techniques. They were a logical choice as a school wide strategy.

Another example of a school wide strategy is the use of think-alouds (Duffy, Roehler, and Herrmann, 1988), a process wherein teachers read a portion of text, pause, and verbally share their thinking process. When teachers do this, they are in essence making thinking "public." The teacher models what is going on in their head. The development of think-alouds takes into account the fact that when most people read, they actively think about what they are reading. They question, clarify, and resolve what they don't understand. However, many readers, particularly struggling readers, do not mentally engage in these thinking processes. When a teacher conducts a think-aloud, it can help all students make greater connections and deepen understanding.

There are numerous other instructional strategies that could be selected as school wide strategies based upon an analysis of data. Each Northview building staff studied student data to determine common literacy needs. In their professional conversations, teachers inquired of each other about the most effective practice, "How did you do that? Why did you teach those strategies? I never thought of teaching that. Can you share the strategy with me?" These are some of the comments heard frequently in PLC groups and department meetings. Though sometimes posed as a simple question, teachers were beginning to experience the power of consistency.

Each building determined three to five school wide strategies. Everyone had a voice and a vote. Dr. Julia Reynolds, a local college professor and critical friend, said, "Staff realize if they consistently use common practices it will benefit students who move from class to class and grade to grade."

Northview High School adopted the following school wide literacy strategies:

- content vocabulary instruction—graphic organizers and Foldables ®

- sustained silent reading (SSR)

- words-of-the-week (vocabulary development program for all students Grades 9-12)

- and school wide writing prompts.

"The work of the high school provides a model for other schools," Dr. Reynolds suggests. "Their success can be attributed to consistency in:

- staff analyzing data to determine student learning needs.

- teachers engaging in professional conversations to improve instruction.

- teams partnering with the building principal to create job-embedded adult learning opportunities.

- everyone participating in instructional decision making.

- and the school developing external critical friendships."

Northview High School is increasing instructional effectiveness with its common literacy focus and consistent school wide instructional practices. One member of the school literacy team adds, "Thanks to the consistency of our approach, we bond the work of the school together so it's happening everywhere. It ensures that *strategies, practices, and protocols are in place for the benefit of not only the students, but the faculty as well.*"

Staff Conversations

A Conversation with Jim Haveman, High School Science Teacher:

The Power of a Simple Question

The Northview High School science department chairperson, Jim Haveman, commented, "I often wonder how to help my students. I can see that if kids understand vocabulary in science, they will be more successful learning content. It's funny; it's less about understanding science concepts, and more about vocabulary and reading skills. I've heard that the elementary uses something called word walls. I wonder if that would be helpful for my high school science students to be more successful."

A High School Parent Conversation: Foldables®, a School-Wide Strategy That Works

Regardless of grade level or content area, school wide strategies were implemented building wide. Students and parents appreciated this consistent use of literacy strategies.

One high school parent commented that his son used Foldables®, by Dinah Zike, a note taking strategy adopted building-wide. The parent observed his son using a foldable with work from four different subject areas.

Before, we never saw Josh's notebooks or study notes. Now, he actually is required to have these Foldables®, to take notes in class and we find he uses them to do homework and study for tests. It is so helpful that teachers studied this technique, determined that it would help kids learn better, and are actually using it in most of his classes. My son would never be caught dead making or studying from something like this. But he does because he sees other kids using it. The great thing is that kids have a learning tool to reinforce instruction. It doesn't matter the class or subject; it is consistent; and all his teachers are using it. It also helps parents since we can see what our son is learning.

With the common strategies, teachers commented that things felt different. They appreciated the support that they were getting from each other, administrators, coaches, and from the district. They were accountable to determine the strategies and use them. Time was given to learn and observe modeling of strategies. A variety of resources was made available to support their efforts, including the help of instructional coaches. The literacy initiative was tight and consistent. The goal was that no one would fall through the cracks—no student and no teacher.

The destination of literacy provided Northview with a newfound opportunity. Never before had the staff been on the same page instructionally. This provided a collective strength to focus on each and every student's achievement, not because it was mandated, but because the mission for them as educators was to achieve greater results. Teachers identified student literacy needs and used them to improve their instructional practices. It was one small step for each and every teacher, but one giant leap for the entire system.

Whether we are in our classroom or on a plane, consistent practices ensure a steady ride. We all know what to expect. That builds trust. Consistency of practice, regardless of the setting, helps us get where we are going.

"Take-Aways"

• *Since the vision and mission are so important, how do we engender pervasive stakeholder ownership?*

• *How does the consistent implementation of an instructional framework strengthen our instructional program?*

• *Who benefits from the consistent application of shared strategies? Why?*

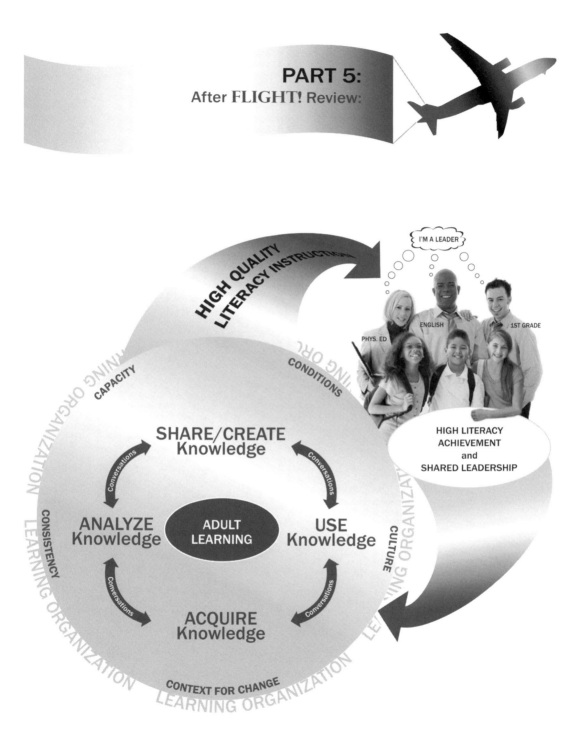

This simple graphic represents the impact of the three fields of work: literacy, adult learning, and systems thinking. It shows the integration of work within the entire school system that results in increased literacy achievement, shared leadership, and transformation to a learning organization. The learning of the students, staff, and system provides energy for continual growth.

Chapter 17

Landing With Impact

Tough Questions:

- What does it take to improve instruction?
- What is a learning organization?
- How do roles change in a learning organization?

Key Learning Principles:

- Good instruction works.
- An identity of shared leadership develops when staff use their voices to share what they know and participate in decision making.

Main Ideas:

- The fields of literacy instruction, adult learning, and systems thinking require attention, commitment, and ongoing work.
- The dynamic between the three fields can transform a school system into a learning organization.
- Learning organizations may change the way we think about and practice our profession.

*A*t the end of our FLIGHT! we disembark to our destination while our pilot and copilot remain in the cockpit. It is a requirement that they complete an After FLIGHT! Review process. In an After FLIGHT! Review, the team records and analyzes the data, so that the next FLIGHT! is as successful.

Just like the pilot, we authors conducted an "After FLIGHT! Review" to determine the impact of our work. An After Action Review (AAR), originally developed by the Army to improve battlefield tactics, has the goal of improving future performance. Like the Learning Cycle (chapter 9) AAR is a simple process to determine the lessons learned from a chosen strategy and action. It makes tacit knowledge explicit, giving all members of the team access to it. It gives participants an opportunity to reflect on their work so that the next time, they can achieve even greater success.

Our After FLIGHT! Review asks three questions:

- What was supposed to happen?
- What happened?
- What worked?

These three questions will be applied to the three fields of literacy, adult learning, and systems thinking that emerged from the partnership work over seven years in Northview. These fields give form and function to the mission and vision; they are dynamic and adaptable to the needs of the moment. These fields provide arenas wherein we practice our intentions and develop our future. According to Wheatley (1992, p. 56), "Once we create them (fields), once we invest resources in putting them out there, they will sustain themselves."

Although the After FLIGHT! Review considers the three fields of work in Northview Public Schools separately, it is essential to recognize that these three fields were continually interrelated and influencing one another. It is tempting to suggest a direct correlation between

n; ability to demonstrate an accomplishment of some kind for which the outcome involves a learning experience

Student Art Work by Kara D.

each of the fields and a specific impact. However, in systems work, both learning and progress are achieved through connections and integration. We cannot attribute progress to one field of work without acknowledging the influence of the other two fields.

The impact of the three fields is:

- *Student achievement in literacy* rose steadily at the same time that poverty rates were climbing.

- Staff developed an identity of *shared leadership*.

- The school system began to *operate as a learning organization.*

After Flight Review in the Field of Literacy

WHAT WAS SUPPOSED TO HAPPEN IN THE FIELD OF LITERACY?

The seven-year partnership with The Ball Foundation was forged to provide support for Northview's pursuit of increased student achievement. Partnership goals included using data to improve instruction and learning. Three years into the partnership it became clear that the entire K-12 staff needed to focus on literacy instruction in all content areas.

WHAT HAPPENED IN THE FIELD OF LITERACY?

Student Literacy Achievement Increases

The most striking impact of the seven-year Northview-Ball Foundation partnership was the fact that literacy achievement scores in Northview rose despite increased levels of poverty in all of its schools. As described at the outset of the book, scores for Grades 4, 7, and 11 showed gains. On average, 4th graders posted scores 15 percentage points higher than 4th graders statewide, and scores reflected 91%-93.8% proficiency for the past five years tracked.

Northview's 7th grade scores reflected a similar story. Over the seven years of the partnership, scores rose 32 percentage points to reach 83%-88% proficiency levels. 11th grade students in Northview outperformed state-wide peers by 8 percentage points. Most years' scores showed consistently high proficiency levels between 81% and 88% proficiency.

A New Priority Is Placed on Literacy Instruction

Especially significant in the field of literacy was the new priority that was placed on instruction in Northview. With the literacy focus, Northview elevated its view of instructional practice. Michael Schmoker in *Results Now: How We Can Achieve Unprecedented Improvements in Teaching and Learning* (2006) asks us to dream of a preferred future when students are well prepared for school, the dropout rates and the achievement gaps are shrinking, and there is a pervasive sense of hope for schools. He asks us to "Imagine a time in the future . . ." (when the above improvements are in place), and says, "All of these improvements result from a new candor that has emerged in education and a willingness to see that historic improvement isn't about 'reform' but something much simpler: a tough, honest self-examination of the prevailing culture and practices of public schools, and a dramatic turn toward a singular and straightforward *focus on instruction*" (p. 2).

This dramatic shift occurred with staff in grade level groups, in PLC's, and in department meetings throughout the system. Conversations now turned, more so than ever before, to instruction:

- How are we teaching?

- Can we do better?

- How are you teaching that particular lesson?

- What results are you getting?

- Will you share your instructional ideas with me?

- What multiple data sets will help inform my instruction?

- Is what I am doing instructionally working with my students?

These types of questions echoed throughout the system, questions about literacy instruction and best practices. Schmoker adds, "the single greatest determinant of learning is not socioeconomic factors or funding levels. It is instruction" (p. 7). Schmoker was right. It took tough, honest self-examination of the culture and practices of our schools, which were the catalyst for a straightforward focus on literacy instruction.

WHAT WORKED IN THE FIELD OF LITERACY?

Improved Instruction with a Literacy Focus

Staff Conversations

A Conversation with Connie Petter, District Learning Consultant:

"We Don't Just Wish for Success"

"Our teachers work like scientists to analyze their literacy instruction to make sure it's effective. They work collaboratively to discuss what works, what is most effective, and what isn't working. They share instructional ideas. Before we just patted ourselves on the back when we did well, or felt badly when we didn't. You can't just have generic wishes for success. When teachers come together and put instructional literacy practices under the microscope they break down how they can improve that practice. We continually have to respond to what the data is telling us and we make changes as a result. We now realize we have to calendar those opportunities to really analyze what we are doing in our instruction and its impact on student achievement. Again, we don't just wish for success."

Sharing of Best Practices

Staff Conversations

A Staff Conversation with Judy Care:

"We are spreading literacy best practices all over the district"

Judy Care, then Director of Instruction for Northview, talks about numerous literacy opportunities available to teachers. "We purchased resources for teachers to learn about best practices and they studied the work of literacy experts. They learned about practices that highly

(continued)

correlate with student achievement including Marzano's research, and Fisher and Frey's work related to K-12 literacy.

"The Language Arts and Literacy Leadership Group fostered book clubs, strategy demonstrations, and voluntary summer workshops. They initiated a literacy coaching network cultivating literacy leaders throughout the district. The coaches and literacy leaders modeled consistent practices for teachers. They were available to support teachers instructionally and teachers are reporting great results. One key factor in helping teachers understand best practices is our adoption of the K-12 literacy framework. Common practices and vocabulary unite the staff."

Another advantage of adoption of a Literacy Framework was the increased dose of reading and writing. By identifying literacy as the district's primary focus, teachers could impact students' learning across content areas. According to Michael Schmoker, "Generous amounts of close, purposeful reading, rereading, writing, and talking, as underemphasized as they are in K-12 education, are the essence of authentic literacy. These simple activities are the foundation for a trained, powerful mind—and a promising future. They are the way up and out—of boredom, poverty, and intellectual inadequacy. And they're the ticket to ensuring that record numbers of minority and disadvantaged youngsters attend and graduate from college" (2006, p. 53).

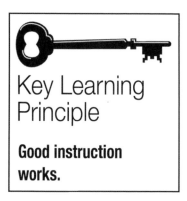

Key Learning Principle

Good instruction works.

The system's leadership, along with staff at all levels, clearly communicated why the literacy focus was so crucial. With the district's changing demographics and increasing poverty levels, it made more sense than ever. Staff continued to put in place supports and structures that would help achieve the literacy focus.

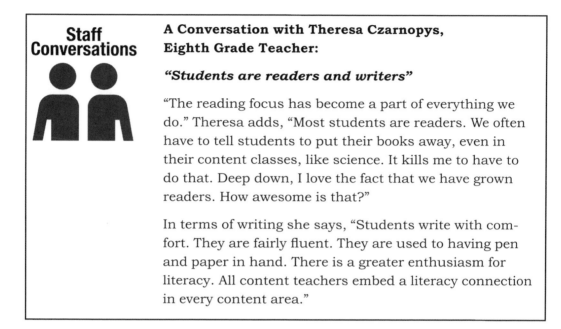

Staff Conversations

A Conversation with Theresa Czarnopys, Eighth Grade Teacher:

"Students are readers and writers"

"The reading focus has become a part of everything we do." Theresa adds, "Most students are readers. We often have to tell students to put their books away, even in their content classes, like science. It kills me to have to do that. Deep down, I love the fact that we have grown readers. How awesome is that?"

In terms of writing she says, "Students write with comfort. They are fairly fluent. They are used to having pen and paper in hand. There is a greater enthusiasm for literacy. All content teachers embed a literacy connection in every content area."

An Innovative Method of Professional Development: We Cultivate Our Own Experts

With a focus on literacy instruction, teachers came to believe that they could be experts for one another. Less emphasis was placed on bringing in "stand and deliver" experts, those presenters who drive or fly in for one day, and head out of town when the professional development day is over.

In the foreword of *Whatever It Takes: How Professional Learning Communities Respond When Kids Don't Learn* (DuFour, DuFour, Eaker, Karhanek, 2004, p. xv.), the authors include an insight from Michael Fullan. They relate, "Michael Fullan has written about the 'culture of dependency' among school personnel—that we tend to wait for solutions from the outside. These authors tell us that instead of looking 'out the window,' that we need to look 'in the mirror' at what we can do right now, always with the expectation of making discernible progress in the short *and* the long term. Although having money is terrific, the brutal fact is that it is no substitute for the actions and effort most apt to improve teaching and learning."

Staff had the opportunity to improve their instructional practice by viewing demonstration lessons modeled by a literacy coach or willing colleague. The lesson modeled a literacy strategy and took place with actual students in a classroom, while groups of teachers watched seated around the perimeter of the room. After the lesson, the group of teacher observers was escorted to a conference room down the hall. The coach might ask, "Well, what did you see?" At times the coach may share ideas, but first insists upon debriefing the lesson via discussion, inquiry, and dialogue. Teachers comment, question, express their concerns, wonderings, and ideas.

Combining observation of a literacy strategy demonstration with a structured debrief fostered adults' learning about their instructional practice. The coach urged teachers to pair what they had seen with what they already knew to upgrade their instruction.

Staff Conversations

Staff Conversations with Kathy Van Dessel and Kelly Johnston, Elementary Teachers:

"The Best Literacy Learning"

Kathy Van Dessel, fourth grade teacher, talked about the importance of modeling, and taking time to make sure everyone has a shared understanding of common vocabulary and literacy strategies. "We can't do that if we don't take the time to dialogue together." She said, "It is the rich conversations about instructional practice with colleagues that make each of us better."

Kelly Johnston, a first grade teacher, explains, "We learn by seeing others actually applying knowledge and skills; it has brought the learning to life. Teachers are reporting this observation/debrief to be the best professional development they have ever participated in. It is job-embedded, links to the data on our students, and offers teachers support." Kelly continues, "We have a real need for the learning, and we have the time to *make the learning our own* through the conversation and debrief afterwards. We have begun to realize we can be experts to each other—we can help each other learn."

After FLIGHT! Review in the Field of Adult Learning:

WHAT WAS SUPPPOSED TO HAPPEN?

When we began the partnership with The Ball Foundation, we expected three results relative to the learning of adults:

- Staff would have the capability to use data to make instructional decisions.

- Staff would share and create best practices in the delivery of the curriculum.

- Staff would engage in collaborative, professional conversations to improve student achievement.

As the partnership progressed the need to develop staff as learners became an important focus of the district's work. It was obvious that the staff could not meet the above expectations without a structure for professional learning. This focus on adult learning included the administrative team.

WHAT HAPPENED IN THE FIELD OF ADULT LEARNING?

Sharing Leadership

Never before had Northview intentionally developed the capacity for teachers and administrators to share leadership so broadly. Administrators realized that leadership must *not* be relegated to administrators alone. Shared leadership was like a cluster of balloons. As the grip is loosened, each balloon has the ability to fly higher. The less the administrators held onto it, the more staff could take Flight! This understanding transformed the district and resulted in expanded leadership opportunities for staff.

Staff Conversations

A Conversation with Megan Ballmer, third grade teacher:

"We want to be invited."

"When you invite people in, they are more than happy to serve as leaders. They just want to be invited. It makes people feel valued. Lots more people are on board and

(continued)

getting pulled in because they legitimately know their perspective is heard and they can affect the way things are done. In some places administrators are hesitant to invite teachers to become involved. But in Northview, there is a welcoming spirit. It starts with the Superintendent and goes out from the administrators. You can assume leadership and be as involved as you wish to be.

"New teachers here enjoy respect from the first day of employment. They do not have to prove themselves before they can use their voice and serve in leadership roles. It's important for everyone to have a sense that they are treated as a professional and that they are able to participate and offer their expertise. It's a great open environment."

Collaborating for Instruction

In *Guiding Professional Learning Communities: Inspiration, Challenge, Surprise, and Meaning* (2010, p. 24), Hord and Roussin relate, "Reports in the literature are quite clear about what successful professional learning communities look like and act like. The requirements necessary for such organizational arrangements include the following:

- The collegial and facilitative participation of the principal, who shares leadership and power by engaging staff in decision making

- A shared vision for students' learning that is consistently articulated

- Collective learning and application of solutions that address students' needs

- The visitation and review of teachers' instruction by peers as a learning and feedback activity

- Physical conditions and human capacities that support such an operation

Evidence of the benefits of professional learning communities could readily be found in Northview. Whether staff called their building's collaborative structure a *PLC or team,* the following characteristics existed:

- Teachers believed they could achieve greater results with collaboration versus isolation. Teachers were encouraged and had models to learn from one another.

- Principals promoted shared leadership and welcomed teachers as equal participants in instructional leadership.

- Staff was committed to make sure all students learned; student learning was the goal of all instruction.

- Staff valued professional conversations for purposes of sharing best practices and strategies.

- Literacy leaders and willing staff modeled strategies in each other's classrooms. They had the opportunity to collectively debrief the lesson.

- The district supported PLC's and collaborative structures. They encouraged staff training, provided release time for meeting collaboratively, and established schedules that secured time for collaboration.

Another collaborative process that jump-started a discipline for adult learning in some buildings was Collaborative Analysis of Student Work or "CASL." It was a process that prioritized the role of professional conversations. The book *Collaborative Analysis of Student Work: Improving Teaching and Learning* (2003), by Colton, Langer, and Goff explains, "The Collaborative Analysis of Student Learning (CASL) system is designed to help teachers analyze student work to improve instructional decisions and, thus, students' learning. . . As part of the system, teachers join in a study group to interpret and document students' progress toward local learning standards and reflect upon how students learn as well as upon their own professional growth" (p. 11).

Another dimension of the CASL program is the dialogue between teachers which uses

Student Art Work by Sarah P.

communication skills that "Establish and maintain a safe and trusting environment, and encourage group members to reexamine, clarify, and transform their thinking so that they can help students succeed" (p. 13).

Whatever the structure, staff had multiple opportunities to collaborate, to plan, to learn from one another, and exchange instructional strategies. One high school teacher, new to the district, commented that he learned so much from another veteran colleague in his same department. He respectfully referred to this veteran as the "Queen of English." He also commented, "I would love to see her teach. I know she does so many awesome things to get kids to learn. She is so innovative. It's obvious she puts so much time into each lesson. I just want to learn from her so *my* classroom can benefit from those same strategies."

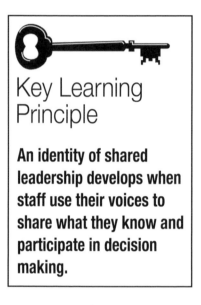

Key Learning Principle

An identity of shared leadership develops when staff use their voices to share what they know and participate in decision making.

With an emphasis on collaboration, new staff members reaped the benefits of being part of a collaborative group that plans together and shares instructional strategies. They learned from the veteran teachers to make instruction more effective. Gone are the days of isolation, the closed classroom, and the one teacher who "holds the secrets to success." Staff valued the time to work together, to learn together, to share knowledge so that all students could benefit.

WHAT WORKED IN THE FIELD OF ADULT LEARNING?

Staff Came To Understand the Power of Collaboration

One of the greatest successes in the field of adult learning was that staff came to understand:

- The value of collaboration

- The purpose of collaborative time

- The focus on instruction as the heart of collaborative time

- The importance of data to PLC or team time

- The role of professional conversations for collaboration.

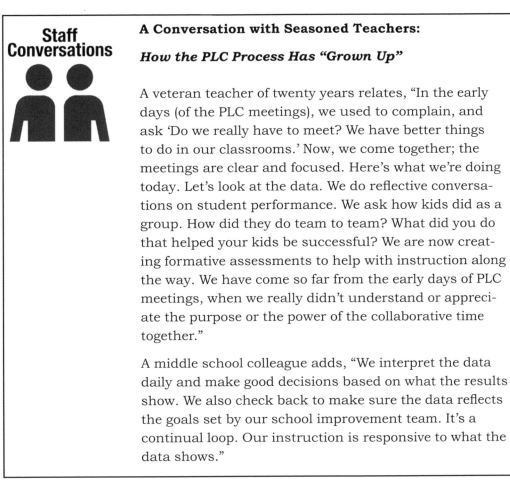

Staff Conversations

A Conversation with Seasoned Teachers:

How the PLC Process Has "Grown Up"

A veteran teacher of twenty years relates, "In the early days (of the PLC meetings), we used to complain, and ask 'Do we really have to meet? We have better things to do in our classrooms.' Now, we come together; the meetings are clear and focused. Here's what we're doing today. Let's look at the data. We do reflective conversations on student performance. We ask how kids did as a group. How did they do team to team? What did you do that helped your kids be successful? We are now creating formative assessments to help with instruction along the way. We have come so far from the early days of PLC meetings, when we really didn't understand or appreciate the purpose or the power of the collaborative time together."

A middle school colleague adds, "We interpret the data daily and make good decisions based on what the results show. We also check back to make sure the data reflects the goals set by our school improvement team. It's a continual loop. Our instruction is responsive to what the data shows."

Northview intentionally worked on developing *effective* collaborative structures. For administrators and staff, it was an ongoing process to make collaborative time together meaningful and authentic. The process needs to be guided and reviewed with an eye on improving what we are doing. As one middle school teacher stated, "The process is always re-evaluated to see if we can make it better. We try out new ideas and are always exchanging instructional strategies about best practices. We have come to rely on this time to work together."

Design Teams: "A Place at the Table"

In *Leading Minds: An Anatomy of Leadership,* Howard Gardner, uses the phrases "without voice" or "without a place at the table" (p. 295). In Northview, perhaps one of the most significant things that "worked" was that staff was encouraged to share their voices and participate. Because leadership was more readily shared by administrators they could "have a place at the table." One of the processes used in Northview to cultivate such staff leadership was the use of the design team. It came to be standard operating procedure for planning meetings, retreats, and district events.

A key feature of design teams was that participation was open to anyone. It was invitational in the sense that anyone interested was invited to serve on a design team. Design teams operationalize a critical key learning principle: "People only own what they create (Wheatley, 1992) or find meaningful."

Northview discovered that administrators cannot lead alone. They came to realize that when administrators invite staff participation in design teams, they are building leadership partnerships. Staff has the opportunity to contribute their expertise. They are part of the decision making. They *own* the work they help create. They are valued as professionals. It is a real ticket for success.

WHAT WAS SUPPOSED TO HAPPEN IN THE FIELD OF SYSTEMS THINKING?

At the outset of the partnership work in Northview, a big question was how we might use the school system to foster student learning. Our partners, The Ball Foundation, had collaborated in writing a text, *Using What We Have to Get the Schools We Need* (1995), that challenged us to think about our effectiveness using the following terms:

- focus
- alignment
- data-driven decision making
- learning
- and innovation and dissemination.

We began to view our work as less about imparting content knowledge and skills, and more about the processes of learning in a social setting. It took much reflection and conversation to understand how these concepts could be integrated to form a picture of a system that learns. In fact the relationships among these concepts often became apparent only after we had implemented them in authentic work.

Gradually we began to understand systems thinking and its dynamic nature. We saw that these original concepts of focus, alignment, data-driven decision making, learning, innovation, and dissemination grew a system's capacity to anticipate and respond to change. They became a springboard in helping us define the facets of a system that we could intentionally align in support of student, adult, and organizational learning. We integrated the foundation's concepts with the systems thinking of Senge (1990), Wheatley (1992) and The Harvard Change model (Wagner, Kegan, Lahey, Lemons, Garnier, Helsing, Howell, Thurber Rasmussen, 2006). From this amalgamation in our authentic work, we discerned five essential components of a system:

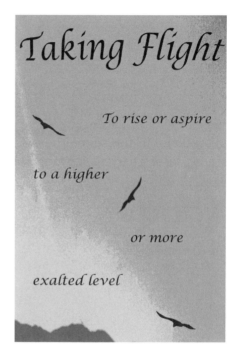

Student Art Work by Sarah P.

- Context for Change

- Conditions

- Culture

- Capacity

- Consistency

WHAT HAPPENED IN THE FIELD OF SYSTEMS THINKING?

Staff Sees Connections, and Information Flows Freely

According to Senge (1994) systems thinking is a way of seeing all the facets of a school district as interconnected. These parts and pieces are "all oriented to looking at the interrelatedness of forces, and seeing them as part of a common process" (p. 89). Systems thinking is a powerful way to think about the complex milieu in which we work. Wheatley (1992) would say that this process is fed by information whose source, in large part, are the participants of the district. When systems thinking is employed there is no "top-down or bottom-up" (Senge, 1994, p. 89); instead participation occurs at all levels based on a shared understanding of common purpose.

The reader will note in Chapter 1 that staff described themselves as working well together with a high level of satisfaction to increase student learning. Principals made collaboration a priority for their staffs and for their own growth as learning leaders. Collectively principals and teachers developed a positive, working environment wherein everyone understood their role relative to the vision, and information flowed freely. This is an example of systems work.

Staff Conversations

A Conversation with Cindi O'Connor, Elementary Principal:

A Reflection on Contributions as a Learning Leader

"Instructional leadership, to me, really becomes a 'contribution' when it results in sustainable systems that produce student achievement over time. I see my work as an instructional leader to provide an environment for staff to gain insights from student data and to, in turn, be the instructional leaders for their teams. I hope that by bringing best practices, enabling teachers to seek best practices, and finding ways to locate resources within a structure that is a 'system,' it will continue to grow and evolve to meet student needs."

Senge (1994) quotes Pat Walls, a Federal Express managing director, who used systems thinking to bring unprecedented improvements to customer relations, "When you trace back the stories, you find out that all this change came from hundreds of little things that individuals were doing differently. It's like the old expression, 'You are what you eat.' If you start thinking differently, you see things differently. And all your actions start to change" (p. 88). All of the different knowledge sets, when brought together, provide a treasure trove of differences which can be mined for new decisions in support of learning.

Staff is Involved in Decision Making

Involving the entire staff in decision making enabled the Northview system to tap hundreds of differing perspectives. From "making time for instruction" to aligning its goals and budget to the district literacy focus, teachers used their own knowledge to make important decisions. They sought information (data) they needed for their instruction and for building relationships, not only with colleagues but also with students and parents. Their data also informed them of their own learning needs which, as a staff, they began to design and execute.

Staff Conversations

A Conversation with Robin Paredez:

Systems Thinking Shifts My Approach to My Profession

"With the system's use of data, I experienced a dramatic pedagogical shift from teaching to learning. Through data warehousing we were able to access varied, valuable information to assist our quest for greater student learning."

Staff "Stand Together" With Focus and Consistency

Both the literacy and instructional frameworks brought consistency to professional practice with shared vocabulary and common understandings. Combined with a commonly held vision these frameworks brought increased focus and predictability to the professional life of the entire district. Senge (1994) suggests that "a system is a perceived whole whose elements 'hang together' because they continually affect each other over time and operate toward a common purpose." The word "system" descends from the Greek verb *sunistanai* which originally meant "to cause to stand together."

WHAT WORKED IN THE FIELD OF SYSTEMS THINKING?

Staff Functions as a Learning Organization

When a system deliberately sets itself up to learn in order to create its preferred future, it practices tenets of a learning organization. What is a learning organization? There doesn't appear to be common agreement on the definition of a learning organization. However, there are common themes as evidenced in the following three definitions:

- Learning organizations [are] organizations where people continually expand their capacity to create the results they truly desire, where new and expansive patterns of thinking are nurtured, where collective aspiration is set free, and where people are continually learning to see the whole together (Senge, 1990).

- The Learning Company is a vision of what might be possible. It is not brought about simply by training individuals; it can only happen as a result of learning at the whole organization level. A learning company is an organization that facilitates the learning of all its members and continuously transforms itself (Pedler, Burgoyne, and Boydell, 1996).

- Learning organizations are characterized by total employee involvement in a process of collaboratively conducted, collectively accountable change directed towards shared values or principles (Watkins and Marsick, 1992: 118).

Common to all of these definitions is the idea that "learning is valuable, continuous, and most effective when shared and that every experience is an opportunity to learn" (Kerka, 1995).

Kerka (1995) suggests that learning organizations are identifiable by the following characteristics:

- Use learning to reach their goals.

- Link individual performance with organizational performance.

- Foster inquiry and dialogue, making it safe for people to share openly and take risks.

- Embrace creative tension as a source of energy and renewal.

- Are continuously aware of and interact with their environment.

Given the staff's reflections on their learning in the three fields of work, we conclude that the partnership work resulted in the school system operating as a learning organization. This conclusion is supported by the argument of Finger and Brand (1999) who suggest that a learning organization needs to attend to the structures and the organization of the work as well as the culture and processes. The model that represents the project work in *Taking Flight to Literacy and Leadership!* does just that. It also satisfies another imperative that a link is intentionally forged between individual and collective learning and the organization's strategic objectives (Smith, 2001).

Staff Shifts to Being Teachers and Learners

As a learning organization, the focus of our work has shifted. In order to make the difference we all set out to accomplish, we have shifted from being teachers to becoming teachers and learners. We think differently. It is a more expansive way to view the world. We have come out of our classrooms to share and create best practices. We understand that we are each responsible to be a contributing part of a larger whole. We now collectively ground our decisions on what we know and imagine what can be. Senge (1990) implies that we are changing not only what we think about, but also how we go about thinking. Accordingly he suggests that "learning organizations may be a tool not just for the evolution of organizations, but for the evolution of intelligence" (p. 367).

Senge (1994, p. 4) reminds us, "How do I fix things? You can't just fix things, at least not permanently. You can apply theories, methods, and tools, increasing your own skills in the process. You can find and instill new guiding ideas. And you can experiment with redesigning your organization's infrastructure. If you proceed in all these ways, you can gradually evolve a new type of organization. It will be able to deal with the problems and opportunities of today and invest in its capacity to embrace tomorrow, because its members are continually focused on enhancing and expanding their collective awareness and capabilities. You can create, in other words, an organization which can learn."

Becoming a learning organization is "challenging" work that stretches our minds and our spirits. It is "big" work that touches everyone in the school system. It is the work of learning, of growing, and of making a difference.

Conclusion

While the seven-year partnership has come to an end, the Northview success story continues. The authors take pride in the work staff, administrators, students, and the community did to embrace the process of change in their FLIGHT! to high literacy achievement for all students.

A FLIGHT! to literacy, shared leadership, and learning organization status is one that can be taken by *any* district. It is our hope that our successes and struggles provide one district's example of what intentional systems work can do to foster achievement for all students. As we embarked on this FLIGHT! we did so from a philosophy that uses bold steps to create a preferred future.

As you board *your* plane for your own journey, we invite you to take along the *stories* of these practitioners to guide your path. We suggest you pack the *key learning principles* that may be runway lights for your work. We recommend you use the *tough questions* as an air-traffic controller would check and recheck flight details. We urge you to be guided by what is *in* you, and *in your peers*.

As Orville and Wilbur's persistence reminds us, we must be willing to try, and try, and try again with the faith and knowledge that our collaborative efforts on behalf of students will be successful. We encourage you to take *your own bold steps* in order to create the best future for all those students you serve.

Now, it's time for you to *"Take FLIGHT!"*

Student Art Work by Josh D.V.

References

Allington, R.L. (2009). *What really matters in response to intervention: Research-based designs.* Boston: Allyn & Bacon.

Argyris, C., & Schon, D. (1974). *Theory in practice: Increasing professional effectiveness.* San Francisco: Jossey-Bass.

Bennis, W., & Nanus, B. (1985). *Leaders: The strategies for taking charge.* New York: Harper and Row.

Blasé, J., & Kirby, P.C. (1992). *The power of praise—a strategy for effective principals.* NASSP Bulletin.

Booth, D., & Rowsell, J. (2002). *The literacy principal: Leading, supporting, and assessing literacy initiatives for reading and writing.* Markham, Ontario, Canada: Pembroke Publishers.

Boushey, G., & Moser, J. (2006). *The daily five: Fostering literacy independence in the elementary grades.* Portland, ME: Stenhouse.

Bromley, K., Irwin-DeVitis, L., & Modlo, M. (1995). *Graphic organizers: Visual strategies for active learning.* Jefferson City, MO: Scholastic Professional Books.

Brookfield, S. D. (1983). *Adult learners, adult education and the community.* Oxford, England: Milton Keynes, Open University Press.

Chappuis, S., Chappuis, J., & Stiggins, R. (2009). Supporting teacher learning teams. *Educational Leadership Journal, 66*(5), 60.

Collins, J. (2001). *Good to great: Why some companies make the leap . . . and others don't.* New York: HarperCollins.

Colton, A., Langer, G., Goff, L., (2003). *Collaborative Analysis of Student Work.* Alexandria, VA: Association for Supervision and Curriculum Development.

The Consortium on Productivity in the Schools. (1995). *Using what we have to get the schools we need.* New York, NY: Columbia University.

Conzemius, A., O'Neill, J. (2001). *Building shared responsibility for student learning.* Alexandria, VA: Association for Supervision and Curriculum Development.

Cooperrider, D. (2000). *Appreciative inquiry: Rethinking human organizations through positive theory of change.* Champaign, IL: Stopes Publishing LLC.

Costa, A., Garmston, R., Ellison, J., Hayes, C. (2005). *Cognitive coaching: Foundation seminar learning guide.* Highlands Ranch, CO: Center for Cognitive Coaching.

Covey, S. (1992). *Principle-centered leadership.* New York: Fireside.

Covey, S. (2003). *The seven habits of highly effective people.* New York: Simon & Schuster.

Duffy, G.G., Roehler, L., & Hermann, B.A. (1988). Modeling mental processes helps poor readers become more strategic. *The Reading Teacher, 41,* 762-7.

DuFour, R., DuFour, R., Eaker, R. (2008). *Revisiting professional learning communities at work: New insights for improving schools.* Bloomington, IN: Solution Tree Press.

DuFour, R., DuFour, R., Eaker, R., & Karhanek, G. (2004). *Whatever it takes: How professional learning communities respond when kids don't learn.* Bloomington, IN: Solution Tree Press.

DuFour, R., & Eaker, R. (1998). *Professional learning communities at work: Best practice for enhancing student achievement,* Bloomington, IN: Solution Tree Press.

DuFour, R., & Marzano, R. (2009). High-leverage strategies for principal leadership. *Educational Leadership Journal, 66*(5), 62-8.

Education Week. (2009). *The Obama education plan: An Education Week guide.* San Francisco, CA: Jossey-Bass.

Evans, R. (1996). *The human side of school change: Reform, resistance and the real-life problems of innovation.* Hoboken, NJ: John Wiley & Sons.

Finger, M., & Brand, S.B. (1999). "The concept of the 'learning organization' applied to the transformation of the public section" in Smith, M.K. (5/11/2009). The learning organization: The encyclopedia of informal education. Retrieved from http://www.infed.org/biblio/learning-organization.htm.

Fisher, D., Brozo, W.G., Frey, N., & Ivey, G. (2007). *50 content strategies for adolescent literacy.* Upper Saddle River, NJ: Pearson Education, Inc.

Fisher, D., & Frey, N. (2007). Implementing a schoolwide literacy framework: Improving achievement in an urban elementary school. *Reading Teacher, 61*(1), 32-43.

Fisher, D., & Frey, N. (2004). *Improving adolescent literacy: Strategies that work.* Upper Saddle River, NJ: Pearson Education, Inc.

Fisher, D., Frey, N., & Williams, D. (2002, November). Seven literacy strategies that work. *Educational Leadership Journal, 60*(3), 70-73.

Frey, N., & Fisher, D. (2006). *Language arts workshop: Purposeful reading and writing instruction.* Upper Saddle River, NJ: Pearson Education, Inc.

Fullan, M. (2005). *Leadership and sustainability: System thinkers in action.* Thousand Oaks, CA: Corwin Press.

Fullan, M., Hill, P., & Crévola, C. (2006). *Breakthrough.* Thousand Oaks, CA: Corwin Press.

Gardner, H. (1995). *Leading minds: The anatomy of leadership.* New York: Basic Books.

Garmston, R., & Wellman, B. (2002). *The adaptive school: Developing and facilitating collaborative groups,* 4th ed. El Dorado Hills, CA: Four Hats Seminars, Inc.

Gerard, G., & Ellinor, L. (2001). *Dialogue at work: Skills for leveraging collective understanding.* Waltham, ME: Pegasus Communications, Inc.

Getzels, J., & Guba, E. (1954). Role, role conflict and effectiveness: An empirical study, *American Sociological Review.*

Gladwell, M. (2005). *Blink: The power of thinking without thinking.* New York: Little, Brown and Company.

Goodman, A. (2005, December). The middle school high five: Strategies can triumph. *Voices from the middle, 13*(2), 12.

Gregerman, A. (2007, November). Rediscovering the essence of learning. *Chief Learning Officer, 6*(11), 23.

Hammond, S., & Hall, J. (1998). What is appreciative inquiry? *Inner Edge Newsletter*, 20-1. Retrieved from www.gaacademiccoach.com

Heifitz, R. (1994). *Leadership without easy answers.* Cambridge, MA: The Belknap Press of Harvard University Press.

Heifitz, R., & Linsky, M. (2002). *Leadership on the line.* Boston, MA: Harvard Business School Publishing.

Hinkin, T. (2001). The influence of individual characteristics and the work environment on varying levels of training outcomes. *Human Resource Development Quarterly, 12*(1), 5-23.

Hodgkinson, C. (1991). *Educational leadership: The moral art.* Albany, NY: State University of New York Press.

Hoerr, T.R. (2009). How book groups bring change. *Educational Leadership Journal, 66*(5), 80.

Hord, S.M., & Roussin, J.L. (2010). *Guiding professional learning communities: Inspiration, challenge, surprise, and meaning.* Thousand Oaks, CA: Corwin Press.

Houston, P. (2004). *Comments from the President,* American Association of School Administrators.

Hubbard, R., & Power, B. (1998). *The art of classroom inquiry.* Portsmouth, NH: Heinemann.

Ivey, G., & Fisher, D. (2005). Learning from what doesn't work. *Educational Leadership Journal, 63*(2), 8-14.

Jolly, A. (2008). The evolution of a professional learning team. *Educational Leadership Journal, 12*(2), 3.

Jones, R. (2006, Nov.) Literacy: The next generation. American School Board Journal, 32-5.

Joyce, B., & Showers, B. (1995). *Student achievement through staff development: Fundamentals of school renewal,* 2nd ed. White Plains, NY: Longman Publishers.

Kent Intermediate Newsletter. (2006). Grand Rapids, MI: Kent Intermediate School District.

Kerka, S. (1995). *The learning organization: Myths and realities.* Washington, DC: Eric Clearinghouse. Retrieved from http://www.infed.org/biblio/learning-organization. htm.

Knowles, M. S., Holton, E. F., & Swanson, R. A. (1998). *The adult learner.* 5th ed. Houston, TX: Gulf Publishing Co.

Knowles, M., Holton III, E., & Swanson, R. (2005). *The adult learner: The definitive classic in adult education and human resource development.* 6th ed. Burlington, MA: Elsevier.

Kolb, D. A. (1984). *Experiential learning: Experience as the source of learning and development.* Englewood Cliffs, NJ: Prentice Hall.

Konarska, K. (2008). *Kent Intermediate School District Newsletter.* Grand Rapids, MI: Kent Intermediate School District.

Learning-org. (2001). *Single or double loop learning: Public dialogue on learning organizations.* Retrieved Dec. 14, 2008, from Learning-org. Website: www.learning-org.com

Lortie, D. (1975). *Schoolteacher: A sociological study.* Chicago: University of Chicago Press.

Luidens, P., & Tabor, M. (1999). *Coaching groups to achieve peak performance.* Grand Rapids, MI: Presented to Kent Intermediate School District.

Marzano, R. J., Pickering, D. J., & Pollock, J. E. (2001). *Classroom instruction that works: Research-based strategies for increasing student achievement.* Alexandria, VA: Association for Curriculum and Supervision.

Marzano, R., & Waters, T. (2005). School district leadership that works: a working paper. Denver, CO: Midcontinent Research Laboratory.

Marzano, R., Waters, T., & McNulty, B. (2005). Balanced leadership, a working paper. Denver, CO: Midcontinent Research Laboratory.

Marzano, R., Waters, T., & McNulty, B. (2005). *School leadership that works.* Alexandria, VA: Association for Curriculum and Supervision.

Matthews, R. (2008, May). How to add storytelling to your toolkit. *Chief Learning Officer, 7*(5), 24.

Maxwell, J.C. (1999). *The 21 indispensable qualities of a leader: Becoming the person others will want to follow.* Nashville, TN: Thomas Nelson.

McAndrew, Donald A. (2005). *Literacy leadership: Six strategies for peoplework.* Newark, NJ: International Reading Assocation.

Morrow, L. M., Gambrell, L. B., & Pressley, M. (Eds.) (2003). *Best practices in literacy instruction* (2nd Edition). New York: Guilford Press.

Nelson, J., Palumbo, J., Cudeiro, A. & Leight, J. (2005). *The power of focus.* USA: Focus on Results.

Newmann, F.M., & Wehlage, G.G., (1993, April). Five standards of authentic instruction. *Authentic Learning, 50*(7), 8-12. Retrieved from http://pdonline.ascd.org/pd_online/diffinstr/el199304_newmann.html

Paxton, P., & Smith, J. (2008). America's trust fall. *The Greater Good,* 15.

Pearson, P.D., & Fielding, L. (1991). Comprehension Instruction. *Handbook of Reading Research, 2,* 815-860. Mahwah, NJ: Erlbaum.

Pedler, M., Burgoyne, J., & Boydell, T. (1991, 1996). *The learning company: A strategy for sustainable development.* London: McGraw-Hill. Retrieved from http://www.infed.org/biblio/learning-organization.htm.

Preskill, H., Torres, R., & Piontek, M. (2006). *Evaluation strategies for communicating and reporting: enhancing learning in organizations.* Thousand Oaks, CA: Sage Publications.

Rasinski, T., Padak, N. (1995). *A handbook of effective literacy: Introduction, effective instruction in literacy.* Kent: Ohio Literacy Resource Center. Retrieved from http://literacy.kent.edu/Oasis/Pubs/lithandbook.html.

Reeves, D. (2006). Challenging the status quo. *Educational Leadership Journal, 63*(8), 32-7, 47-8.

Ricci, J., & Rogers, M. (2003-04). Partnership learning network as a community of practice: A legacy of learning. The *Ball Foundation Review, 4*(1), 1.

Rogers, M.K. (2003-2005). Ongoing training of the Education Initiatives team of The Ball Foundation, Glen Ellyn, IL.

Schein, E. (1969). *Organizational culture and leadership.* San Francisco: Jossey-Bass.

Schmoker, M. (1996). *Results: The key to continuous school improvement.* Alexandria, VA: Alexandria, VA: Association for Supervision and Curriculum Development.

Schmoker, M. (2006). *Results now: How we can achieve unprecedented improvements in teaching and learning.* Alexandria, VA: Association for Supervision and Curriculum Development.

Senge, P. (1990). *The fifth discipline: Art and practice of learning organizations.* New York: Doubleday.

Senge, P., Ross, R., Smith, B., Roberts, C. & Kleiner, A. (1994). *The fifth discipline fieldbook.* NY: Doubleday. Retrieved from http://www.infed.org/biblio/learning-organization.htm

Sergiovanni, T. (1984). Leadership and excellence in schooling. *Educational Leadership Journal, 4*(13).

Sharratt, L., & Fullan, M. (2005, Fall). The school district that did the right things right. *Voices in Urban Education, 9,* Annenberg Institute for School Reform at Brown University.

Smith, M.K. (2001). The learning organization: The encyclopedia of informal education. Retrieved from http://www.infed.org/biblio/learning-organization.htm

Sternberg, E. (2000). *The balance within: The science connecting health and emotions.* New York: W.H. Freeman.

Vaill, P. (1989). *Managing as a performing art.* San Francisco, CA: Jossey-Bass.

Volunteer Pamphlet. (2009). Upper Pinellas County, FL: Literacy Council of Upper Pinellas County, Inc.

Wagner, T. (2003). *Making the grade: Reinventing America's schools.* New York: Routledge Farmer.

Wagner, T., Kegan, R., Lahey, L., Lemons, R., Garnier, J., Helsing, D., Howell, A., & Thurber Rasmussen, H. (2006). *Change leadership: A practical guide to transforming our schools.* San Francisco: Jossey-Bass.

Wahlstrom, D. (1999). *Using data to improve student achievement.* Suffolk, VA: Successline Publications.

Waters, T., & Marzano, R. (2006). School district leadership that works: The effect of superintendent leadership on student achievement, a working paper. Denver, CO: Midcontinent Research Educational Laboratory. Retrieved from www.mcrel.com

Watkins, K., & Marsick, V. (1992). Building the learning organization: A new role for human resource developers. *Studies in Continuing Education, 14*(2) 118, in Smith, M. (2001). The learning organization: The encyclopedia of informal education. Retrieved from http://www.infed.org/biblio/learning-organization.htm

Watkins, K., & Marsick, V. (eds.) (1993). *Sculpting the learning organization. Lessons in the art and science of systematic change.* San Francisco: Jossey-Bass.

Wormeli, R. (2006). *Fair isn't always equal: Assessing and grading in the differentiated classroom.* Portland, ME: Stenhouse Publishers.

Wheatley, M. (1992). *Leadership and the new science.* San Francisco, CA: Berrett-Koehler Publishers.

Wheatley, M. (2002). *Turning to one another.* San Francisco, CA: Berrett-Koehler Publishers.

Wheatley, M., & Rogers, M. (1996). *A simpler way.* San Francisco, CA: Berrett-Koehler Publishers.

York-Barr, J., Sommers, W., Ghere, G., & Montie, J. (2001, April/May). Reflective practice to improve schools. *Tools for Schools, 5*(5), 4.

Yukl, G. (1989). *Leadership in organizations.* Englewood Cliffs, NJ: Prentice-Hall.

Zike, D. (2000). *Dinah Zikes' foldables for grades 1-6: 3D interactive graphic organizers.* New York, NY: Macmillan/McGraw Hill Social Studies Division.

Index